Social Issues
in Literature

Bioethics in
Aldous Huxley's
Brave New World

Other Books in the Social Issues in Literature Series:

Social Issues
in Literature

Bioethics in Aldous Huxley's *Brave New World*

Dedria Bryfonski, Book Editor

GREENHAVEN PRESS
A part of Gale, Cengage Learning

GALE
CENGAGE Learning™

Detroit • New York • San Francisco • New Haven, Conn • Waterville, Maine • London

Christine Nasso, *Publisher*
Elizabeth Des Chenes, *Managing Editor*

For more information, contact:
Greenhaven Press
27500 Drake Rd.
Farmington Hills, MI 48331-3535
Or you can visit our Internet site at gale.cengage.com

For product information and technology assistance, contact us at

Gale Customer Support, 1-800-877-4253
For permission to use material from this text or product, submit all requests online at
www.cengage.com/permissions

Further permissions questions can be emailed to permissionrequest@cengage.com

Articles in Greenhaven Press anthologies are often edited for length to meet page require-ments. In addition, original titles of these works are changed to clearly present the main thesis and to explicitly indicate the author's opinion. Every effort is made to ensure that Greenhaven Press accurately reflects the original intent of the authors. Every effort has been made to trace the owners of copyrighted material.

Cover image by Lipnitzki/Roger Viollet/Getty Images.

LIBRARY OF CONGRESS CATALOGING-IN-PUBLICATION DATA

Bioethics in Aldous Huxley's Brave new world / Dedria Bryfonski, book editor.
    p. cm. -- (Social issues in literature)
  Includes bibliographical references and index.
  ISBN 978-0-7377-4807-9 (hbk.) -- ISBN 978-0-7377-4808-6 (pbk.)
  1. Huxley, Aldous, 1894-1963. Brave new world. 2. Ethics in literature. 3. Biology in literature. 4. Literature and technology. 5. Bioethics--Juvenile literature. I. Bryfonski, Dedria.
  PR6015.U9B6726 2010
  823'.912--dc22
                                                                    2009045212

Printed in the United States of America
2 3 4 5 6 7 14 13 12 11 10

Contents

Chapter 1: Background on Aldous Huxley

Chapter 2: *Brave New World* and Bioethics

Introduction

In a 1961 interview Aldous Huxley explained that his purpose in writing *Brave New World* was to warn of the dangers present if advances in technology and biology got into the wrong hands. He warned of the risk of molding humans "into a kind of uniformity, if you were able to manipulate their genetic background . . . if you had a government unscrupulous enough you could do these things without any doubt. . . . We are getting more and more into a position where these things *can* be achieved. And it's extremely important to realize this, and to take every possible precaution to see they shall *not* be achieved." Such comments indicate that *Brave New World* is not a prophetic novel about what will be, but rather a cautionary tale about what could be.

Although not meant as a prophetic novel, *Brave New World* has proven to be uncannily accurate in many of its scientific predictions. Critics writing in the twenty-first century marvel that Huxley accurately foretold such scientific advances as cloning, test tube babies, and virtual reality, as well as the moral issues that surround these advances. In a review in *Scrutiny* in May 1932, noted scientist Joseph Needham praises *Brave New World*, saying that "*the biology is perfectly right*, and Mr. Huxley has included nothing in his book but what might be regarded as legitimate extrapolations from knowledge and power that we already have." Indeed, in *Brave New World Revisited*, published twenty-six years after *Brave New World*, Huxley's major message is that his predictions were occurring sooner than he had anticipated.

That Huxley was able to be so prescient in *Brave New World* is primarily due to his extraordinary background in science as well as in literature. As critic Philip Thody writes in *Aldous Huxley: A Biographical Introduction*, "[Huxley] certainly knew more science than any other imaginative writer of his generation." As such, he was uniquely suited to write a work that envisioned biological and technological developments while also expressing the moral issues these advances could bring.

Huxley was born into a British family equally distinguished for its scientific and literary achievements. His grandfather, T.H. Huxley, was an eminent supporter of the controversial theory of evolution; his father, Leonard, was an educator, editor, and essayist; his brother Julian was knighted for his work in genetics; his half-brother, Andrew, received the Nobel Prize in 1963 for his work in physiology; his mother, Julia Frances Arnold Huxley, founded Prior's Field School, a girls' boarding school; and his great uncle was the celebrated poet Matthew Arnold.

Although Huxley was only a year old when his grandfather died, the reputation of this scientific giant was a powerful influence on Huxley. Thomas Henry Huxley was a key figure in the scientific revolution and was called "Darwin's Bulldog" for his zealous and persuasive support of the theory of evolution. Biographer Dana Sawyer suggests in *Aldous Huxley: A Biography* that

> the first philosophical worldview that Aldous became aware of was his grandfather's. And many of the philosophical questions he would later wrestle with were direct consequences of theories his grandfather championed, questions his grandfather could not fully have anticipated but nonetheless helped make necessary. In a very real sense, the specifics of Aldous's career and thought were an effect that could be summarized as the sins of the grandfather visited upon the grandson. Thomas Huxley would pull us into the 'Space Age,' and Aldous Huxley would deal with the consequences.

Thody supports the influence Huxley's grandfather had on his writing:

Huxley's realization that the systematic application of technology could lead to a situation where science itself is considered highly dangerous is yet another indication of the fundamental similarity between his attitudes and those of his grandfather. If there was anything to which Thomas Henry Huxley unremittingly devoted his enormous energy, it was the propagation to all members of society of the methods and ideals of scientific inquiry. It was thus consequently as much by respect for family tradition as through personal taste that Aldous Huxley made this destruction of science by its own hand into an important theme in the actual plot of *Brave New World*, and in this he was quite consciously using a novel about the future to comment on current development in his and our society.

With the powerful influence of his grandfather's reputation, it is not surprising that Huxley's early intentions were to study science, become a physician, and specialize in medical research. His plans changed, however, when he was stricken at age seventeen with keratitis punctata, an inflammation of the cornea that caused him to be blinded for eighteen months. After four operations, he regained sight in one of his eyes. His limited vision caused him to give up his boyhood aspirations to become a scientist, and he instead turned to writing.

An interest in science remained with him throughout his life. In *Along the Road*, a book of travel essays, he says that in another life, he would choose to be a scientist. "The only thing that might make me hesitate would be an offer by fate of artistic genius. But even if I could be Shakespeare, I still think I would choose to be Faraday."

He interrupted his literary endeavors in the 1920s to work briefly at the technologically advanced Brunner and Mond chemical plant in Billingham, Teesside, and from these experiences gathered background that would be used in *Brave New World*.

His brother Julian wrote in *Aldous Huxley 1894–1963: A Memorial Volume*, a collection of tributes from friends and associates, that "most people seem to imagine that Aldous came to me for help over the biological facts and ideas he utilized so brilliantly in *Brave New World* and elsewhere in his novels and essays. This was not so. He picked them all up from his miscellaneous reading and from occasional discussions with me and a few other biologists, from which we profited as much as he."

In Huxley's memorial volume, the distinguished British biographer and literary scholar David Cecil summed up the strength that the combination of science and literature played in the artistry of Aldous Huxley,

> In Aldous Huxley's veins flowed the blood of Matthew Arnold and of Thomas Henry Huxley. From both he drew something. Arnold had bequeathed to him a sensitive imagination soaked in the culture of the past, Huxley an adventurous scientific curiosity disciplined by a stern regard for truth. Aldous Huxley did not find it easy to satisfy both sides of his nature; and much of his life was spent in search of a faith. Yet the fact that he combined in himself these two strains was a necessary condition of his achievement and his influence. It enabled him in an especial way to grasp the contemporary predicament.

Influenced by his distinguished relatives, Huxley developed the scientific rigor that enabled him to imagine a biotechnologically advanced "brave new world" and the metaphysical sensitivity to understand the ethical issues that such a world can bring. In *Social Issues in Literature: Bioethics in Aldous Huxley's "Brave New World"* commentators examine bioethical issues in the novel as well as how these issues are being addressed in twenty-first-century America.

Chronology

1894

Aldous Leonard Huxley is born on July 26, the third son of Leonard Huxley and Julia Arnold Huxley, in the village of Godalming, Surrey, England.

1895

Huxley's grandfather, the biologist Thomas Henry Huxley, dies.

1899

Huxley's sister, Margaret, is born.

1901

The Huxley family moves to Prior's Field, Surrey.

1902

Julia Huxley opens a school for girls at Prior's Field.

1903

Aldous Huxley begins attending Hillside School, a preparatory school near Godalming.

1908

In September Huxley enters Eton College on a scholarship. In November his mother dies.

1909

Leonard Huxley moves to Westbourne Square, London.

1910

An attack of keratitis punctata, an eye infection, causes Huxley to withdraw from Eton. He will be nearly blind for over a year and learns Braille.

1912

Leonard Huxley marries Rosalind Bruce.

1913

Huxley enters Balliol College, Oxford.

1914

Huxley's brother Trevenen commits suicide.

1915

Huxley joins a literary circle at Garsington Manor under the sponsorship of Lady Ottoline Morrell, making the acquaintance of T.S. Eliot, Osbert Sitwell, John Middleton Murry, and others. He meets D.H. Lawrence for the first time in London.

1916

Huxley receives a first-class honors degree in English literature from Oxford. His first volume of poems, *The Burning Wheel*, is published. A short story, "Eupompus Gave Splendour to Art by Numbers," is published in *The Palatine Review*.

1917

Huxley takes a teaching post at Eton until February 1919.

1919

Huxley joins the editorial staff of the *Athenaeum* and moves into a flat in Hampstead Hill, London. He marries Maria Nys, a Belgian refugee, on July 10 in Bellem, Belgium.

1920

Huxley publishes *Limbo*, a collection of short stories. Maria Huxley gives birth to a son, Matthew, on April 19. Huxley becomes drama critic for the *Westminster Gazette*. In October he resigns his job on the *Athenaeum* and begins work on *House and Garden*. The Huxleys give up the Hampstead flat in December, and Maria and the baby move to Belgium for the winter.

1921

Huxley's first novel, *Crome Yellow*, is published.

1922

A collection of short stories, *Mortal Coils*, is published.

1923

Antic Hay, a novel, is published. The Huxleys move to Italy.

1925

Those Barren Leaves, a novel, is published. Huxley and his wife take a trip around the world, traveling to India, Southeast Asia, Japan, Hong Kong, and the United States.

1926

The Huxleys return to London in June and then move to the Italian Alps for Matthew's health. Huxley renews his friendship with Lawrence in Florence. *Jesting Pilate*, a travel book, is published.

1928

Point Counter Point, a novel, is published. Matthew Huxley attends a boarding school, Frensham Heights, in Surrey. Aldous and Maria take a house near Paris, in Suresnes.

1929

A collection of essays, *Do What You Will*, is published. Huxley meets Gerald Heard, beginning what will become an important friendship.

1930

The Huxleys buy a house in Sanary-sur-Mer, a seaside village in France. D.H. Lawrence dies, and Huxley edits his letters for publication. *Brief Candles* is published.

1931

Huxley's first play, *The World of Light,* opens at the Royalty Theatre in London and closes after a brief run. *Music at Night,* a collection of essays, is published.

1932

Brave New World is published. *The Letters of D.H. Lawrence,* edited by Huxley, is published.

1933

Leonard Huxley dies. The Huxleys travel to Mexico and Central America.

1934

The Huxleys take a flat in Piccadilly, London. *Beyond the Mexique Bay,* a book recounting Huxley's travels, is published.

1935

Huxley becomes active in the peace movement and gives his first lectures on pacifism and disarmament.

1936

Eyeless in Gaza, a novel, is published.

1937

The Huxleys sail for the United States with Gerald Heard in April. Both Huxley and Heard lecture on peace during a car journey across the United States. *Ends and Means* is published. Huxley meets Swami Prabhavananda and joins the Vedanta movement in California.

1938

Huxley has a screenplay accepted by a film studio in Hollywood, and the Huxleys take a house in Los Angeles. Huxley works for Metro-Goldwyn-Mayer on a script for *Madame Curie.*

1939

After Many a Summer Dies the Swan, a novel, is published. Huxley works on a screenplay for *Pride and Prejudice* for Metro-Goldwyn-Mayer.

1941

Grey Eminence, a biography of the French monk François Leclerc du Tremblay, is published.

1942

The Art of Seeing is published. Huxley works on a screenplay for *Jane Eyre* for Twentieth-Century Fox.

1944

Time Must Have a Stop, a novel, is published.

1945

The Perennial Philosophy, an essay collection, is published. Huxley works on the Walt Disney film *Alice in Wonderland*.

1946

Science, Liberty, and Peace is published.

1948

Huxley writes the screenplay for *A Woman's Vengeance*, based on his story "The Gioconda Smile"; the film is released in February. The stage version, *The Gioconda Smile*, opens at the New Theatre in London in June for a nine-month run. The Huxleys sail to Europe in June, returning to the United States in October. *Ape and Essence*, a novel, is published.

1950

Themes and Variations, a collection of essays, is published.

1952

The Devils of Loudun, a historical book about purported demonic possession in the seventeenth century, is published.

1953

Huxley begins to experiment with psychedelic drugs such as mescaline with Dr. Humphry Osmond.

1954

The Doors of Perception, based on Huxley's drug experiments, is published.

1955

Maria Huxley dies of cancer. *The Genius and the Goddess*, a novel, is published.

1956

Huxley marries Laura Archera in Yuma, Arizona, on March 19. They move to a house in Los Angeles. *Tomorrow and Tomorrow and Tomorrow*, a collection of essays, is published.

1957

Collected Short Stories is published.

1958

Brave New World Revisited, a commentary on *Brave New World*, is published.

1959

Collected Essays is published.

1960

Huxley is diagnosed with cancer.

1961

The Huxley home in Los Angeles is destroyed by fire, consuming his private papers and manuscripts.

1962

Huxley becomes a visiting professor at the University of California, Berkeley. He is elected a Companion of Literature of the British Royal Society of Literature. *Island*, a novel, is published.

1963

Huxley dies of cancer in Los Angeles on November 22. A memorial is held in London on December 17.

Social Issues in Literature

CHAPTER 1

Background on Aldous Huxley

The Life of Aldous Huxley

Johan Heje

Johan Heje (1933–2004) taught literature at Greve Gymnasium, a preparatory school in Denmark, and is the author of Key to Sylvia Plath, "The Bell Jar."

Heje considers Aldous Huxley to be one of the major literary figures of his time. Born into a family with a distinguished background in science and letters, Huxley became accomplished as an essayist, novelist, poet, dramatist, and short-story writer. Heje submits that Huxley was concerned with the issues challenging humanity in the twentieth century both in his essays and in his novels, and Heje describes the latter as being expanded versions of the topics covered in his essays.

For four decades Aldous Huxley was a major figure in the literary mainstream, yet he is now chiefly remembered for a novel that is, by any definition, science fiction. In this respect his position is similar to that of H.G. Wells, who wrote much else besides science fiction but whose reputation has endured as the great pattern-setter for twentieth-century science fiction. Similarly, Huxley's novel *Brave New World* (1932) created a thematic pattern for many subsequent works. Moreover, *Brave New World* was not Huxley's only foray into the futuristic or the fantastic.

Huxley Had a Distinguished Family Background

Aldous Leonard Huxley, born on 26 July 1894 in Surrey, had a family background that predestined him for a distinguished career in the world of science or the world of letters. His fa-

Johan Heje, "Aldous Huxley," in *Dictionary of Literary Biography, vol. 255, British Fantasy and Science-Fiction Writers, 1918–1960*, edited by Darren Harris-Fain, Farmington Hills, MI: The Gale Group, 2002, pp. 97–105. Copyright © 2002 by Gale Group. Reproduced by permission of Gale, a part of Cengage Learning.

ther, Leonard Huxley, a classics master at Charterhouse and later editor of the *Cornhill Magazine*, was the son of T.H. Huxley, the famous biologist and expounder of Darwinism; his mother, Judith Arnold Huxley, was the granddaughter of one of the major educators of the Victorian period, Thomas Arnold of Rugby, and niece of Matthew Arnold. Her sister, Mrs. Humphry Ward, was an admired novelist. Sir Julian Huxley, biologist of world renown and the first director-general of UNESCO, was one of Aldous Huxley's two elder brothers; they also had a younger sister.

Huxley was an avid reader from his earliest years and received an education that befitted his background: Eton and Balliol College, Oxford, from which he graduated in 1916 despite significant damage to his eyesight, caused by keratitis in 1911. While at Oxford he was introduced to Lady Ottoline Morrell, whose country home, Garsington, was a salon for members of England's intellectual elite. Among her house guests Huxley met many people who were, or became, notable scholars or writers. With some of them, most importantly D.H. Lawrence and Bertrand Russell, he formed lasting friendships. At the age of twenty-two he was a published poet, and within a few years he had established a reputation as a promising and provocative essayist, short-story writer, and novelist. He married Belgian-born Maria Nys in 1919, and their son, Matthew, was born in 1920.

Huxley Wrote Novels of Ideas

Garsington obviously provided inspiration for Huxley's first novel, *Crome Yellow* (1921), written much in the manner of Thomas Love Peacock: a group of people are gathered at a country house, and their characters are exposed through various complications in their relationships but most of all through their conversation. Novelties and fads of the early 1920s are glanced at lightheartedly. This novel set a pattern for his next three novels, climaxing in *Point Counter Point*

(1928); certain themes and character types reappeared in new disguises, but the canvas in these novels grew larger, and the satire often more virulent. Always witty and erudite, Huxley came to represent a postwar generation disenchanted with the beliefs and standards of the prewar era, more or less sincerely testing out new mindsets. Though he experimented with increasingly complex forms of narration and tended to view the maladies of his time in psychological rather than sociopolitical terms, he was, and remained, above all concerned with ideas. His novels are, in a sense, enlarged versions of the essays he wrote throughout his life, providing commentaries on an immense variety of topics. Concerned as he was with the future of humanity in a world of apparently uncontrollable change, he was naturally attracted by the utopian and the science-fiction tale, fictional forms that are basically fueled by ideas and speculation on what those ideas may mean if they are transferred into reality.

Brian W. Aldiss posits in his *Trillion Year Spree: The History of Science Fiction* (1986) that "*Brave New World* is arguably the Western world's most famous science fiction novel." With this novel, which has never been out of print since its first publication in February 1932, Huxley reached a larger public than ever before or after. Most of his other novels seem to have faded along with the time they were written in, but his name is inseparable from this book, which has obtained the status of a classic and has, together with George Orwell's *Nineteen Eighty-Four* (1949) provided a whole frame of reference for half a century of debates on what—with a slight rephrasing of a Huxley essay title—may be called the future of the present. In the history of science fiction it stands out as a seminal work, a model for later cautionary tales set in the future.

A Parody of H.G. Wells

Originally, *Brave New World* appears to have been conceived by Huxley as a light diversion. He had in mind a parody of

Wells's utopias, notably *Men Like Gods* (1923). He had, he said twenty-five years later in a letter to Mrs. Arthur Goldsmith, an American acquaintance, "been having a little fun pulling the leg of H.G. Wells," but then he "got caught up in the excitement of [his] own ideas." Like others of his generation, he was skeptical about the belief in evolutionary progress that had been prominent in the thinking of the late-nineteenth and the early-twentieth centuries and that had been almost personified by Wells. Though some of Wells's utopias are actually anti-utopias, in his later works he seemed able to fall back on the conviction that science and reason would prevail in the end. This belief in the impartiality and inherent benevolence of science and technology was precisely what raised Huxley's doubts. The allure of technology is that it makes life easier; the danger is that science and technology are also tools in a quest for power. *Brave New World* depicts the ultimate technocracy. . . .

Huxley returned to his most famous book on several . . . occasions. When George Orwell's *Nineteen Eighty-Four* appeared in 1949 and invited comparisons with *Brave New World,* Huxley wrote Orwell an appreciative letter but found it doubtful that the "boot-on-the-face" tyranny described by Orwell could endure. Future governments would be more likely to employ the "less arduous" means of control he had envisaged in his own novel. In 1958, twenty-six years after the publication of *Brave New World* and thirteen years after World War II, Huxley took stock in *Brave New World Revisited* and could point to much that seemed to bring his vision of the future closer to reality sooner than he had anticipated. In this series of interconnected essays he dealt with topics such as over-population, overorganization, the subliminal persuasion developed in advertising and visual media, and other trends that seemed to indicate that, to paraphrase Sir Winston Churchill, "never have so many been manipulated so much by so few." The question remained whether the human race, being "moderately gregarious" by nature but not a race of termites, could be educated to value freedom. Or would humans always, as thought by Fyodor Dostoevsky's Grand Inquisitor in his 1879–1880 novel, *The Brothers Karamazov* (a model for Huxley's World Controller), be ready to lay down freedom and say to their rulers, "Make us slaves, but feed us"?

In two of his later novels Huxley included fantastic elements in otherwise realistic settings. In *After Many a Summer* (1939), written shortly after he had settled in California with his wife and son in 1938, speculations on longevity set the stage for a comic-horror conclusion. An eighteenth-century English nobleman is revealed to have discovered a life-prolonging effect from eating the viscera of carp and turns out to be still alive and over two hundred years old, though degenerated into happy apehood. In *Time Must Have a Stop* (1944), a best-seller in the United States, one of the characters, a pleasure-loving libertine, refuses to accept his own death and clings to a somehow ineffectual afterlife, struggling to keep his separate essence from being absorbed by the luminous center of things. These novels show the influence of Huxley's friend Gerald Heard, the British mystic, whose philosophy drew upon Buddhism as well as psychoanalysis. Like all of the novels Huxley published in the 1930s and 1940s, they sparked critical debate and varying assessments.

Ape and Essence Dealt with Nuclear Threat

No mention of the potential of nuclear physics had been made in *Brave New World*—a "failure of foresight," Huxley called this omission in his 1946 foreword, for nuclear technology had been "a popular topic of conversation for years before the book was written." In 1948, when he wrote his second novel set in the future, *Ape and Essence*, his theme was the consequences of atomic warfare. The short novel opens, symbolically, in Hollywood on the day of Mahatma Gandhi's assassination in 1947, but this opening turns out to be only a frame for the actual story, a rejected motion-picture script found in a dumpster. Three or four generations after the destruction of most of the world in an atomic war, an expedition sets out from New Zealand, which was untouched because of its geographic isolation, to explore California, where humanity is presumed to be extinct. That is not the case, but the descendants of the few survivors have regressed into a primitive, apelike existence, scavenging among the ruins of a past civilization. Sex is limited to the annual rutting period, and then as an orgy of violence. Women are despised and contemptuously referred to as "vessels" because they are seen as carriers of the curse that the majority of infants are born deformed. The most deformed babies are killed, and their mothers are cruelly whipped. Logically, Belial is worshiped, for has it not been proven that he has won, and so must be propitiated? Religious rituals, administered by a hierarchy of castrated priests, are depicted in detail as Christianity reversed.

Ape and Essence was not well received. Huxley was accused of morbidity and of indulging in sadistic horrors for their own sake. In hindsight, it is possible to give the novel credit as an early serious treatment of the postnuclear holocaust theme and for warnings that are still pertinent. . . .

Later Mystical Influence

During the last two decades of his life Huxley's writings were to a great extent influenced by his study of Eastern mystics. In *The Perennial Philosophy* (1945), an anthology of quotations with commentary, he tried to define the common core of transcendental philosophy and mystical experience throughout the ages: the perception of the basic oneness of humanity and God, atman and Brahman, underlying all religion. In two controversial books, *The Doors of Perception* (1954) and *Heaven and Hell* (1956), he discussed his own experiments with hallucinogens (mescaline and LSD). Though he found similarities between the states of mind induced by these drugs and the vi-

Aldous Huxley (1894-1963). AP Images.

sions of mystics, he never claimed to have had such visions himself or to have achieved any kind of transcendence, only increased self-knowledge. This admission, and his awareness of the potential negative effects of the drugs he tested, have often been overlooked by critics of these books. He did, however, remain interested in the possibility of a mind-liberating drug without negative side effects.

In his last novel, *Island*, written and published a year before his death of cancer in 1963, he invents such a drug, called moksha [Sanskrit for "liberation"], and in his description of its effects he drew upon his own experiences in *The Doors of Perception*. Moksha is used by the inhabitants of Pala, a fictional island in the Indian Ocean. In the nineteenth century a Scots surgeon had come to Pala to treat the local raja for a tumor, and the two men formed a lifelong friendship. A bond was created between Western science, applied beneficially, and ancient Buddhist religion. A truly utopian community developed, which at the beginning of the novel has existed for about a hundred years. Almost point by point this novel can be viewed as an antithesis to *Brave New World*. The people of Pala live in a network of extended families. Family planning is practiced; genetic improvement is ensured by artificial insemination; sickness and death (going into "the Clear Light") are dealt with communally; aggression is channeled; and children are carefully educated in the spiritual exercises that will make them harmonious, knowledgeable members of the community—all by a discerning application of Western science combined with Eastern spirituality. Humanity is at peace with nature; in one scene a Buddha figure in a living room is encircled by a live cobra. Moksha is used to enhance any experience— from love, to classical music, to the contemplation of the unity of all being. The Western, Manichaean dichotomy of good and evil has been resolved in "the reconciliation of yes and no lived out in total acceptance and the blessed experience of Not-Two."

The utopia is not meant to last, however; Pala is already being infiltrated by multinational oil companies and a mainland dictator wanting to exploit Pala's natural resources. In the end the defenseless Palanese community is simply snuffed out by the brute force of the "Modern World." Only the mynah birds with their parrot-like cry of "Attention"—the first and the last word in the novel—remain as reminders of what has been destroyed.

Island received a tepid reception from reviewers and is rarely ranked among Huxley's best books. The least friendly critics called the islanders brainwashed and found moksha similar to soma. Viewed more objectively, the novel can be regarded as an attempt to popularize ideas that had occupied Huxley for many years but that might easily seem abstruse by clothing them in the garment of fiction. He had been at pains to create a plot and credible characters and to depend on dialogue. *Island*, moreover, harks back to a classical utopian tradition, ranging from Plato, Thomas More, and Francis Bacon to William Morris, Samuel Butler, Edward Bellamy, and Wells, even to the point of letting the protagonist, a spying journalist and later a convert, be shipwrecked on an imaginary island, where the utopian marvels are unfolded—a tradition sometimes deprecated by Huxley. With this novel he, the satirist, had joined the club as a serious-minded member. But despite earnest efforts, he could not escape the didacticism inherent in the genre.

In 1956, after Maria Huxley's death from cancer the year before, Huxley married Laura Archera, a psychotherapist, who shared his commitments to mysticism and experimentation with drugs. These commitments have remained a matter of some controversy without affecting his position as a satirist, a science-fiction writer, a philosopher, a utopian, and a belated polyhistor [a very learned person] with roots in nineteenth-century liberal humanism. His wide-ranging intellect and his untiring search for solutions to the dilemmas facing humanity in the twentieth century continued to surprise and challenge his readers to the end.

Huxley Matured as a Writer When He Found the Theme of Humanism

John Atkins

Writer and literary critic John Atkins (1916-2009) published poems, novels, plays, and several works about authors, among them George Orwell: A Literary and Biographical Study.

In the following selection from his biography of Aldous Huxley, Atkins explains the significance of travel in the development of Huxley's work. Huxley traveled extensively, at first around continental Europe and later around the world. His world trip proved to be momentous, Atkins contends. Prior to this trip, Huxley recognized the shallowness of the social circles he moved in but continued to participate in their rituals. During his trip to the United States, and especially to California, he was appalled by the spiritual emptiness he encountered. He returned from this trip with a new seriousness of purpose that manifested itself in a belief in fundamental spiritual values and an openness to diversity.

Aldous Leonard Huxley was born in 1894, the son of Leonard Huxley, editor of the *Cornhill Magazine*, and the grandson of Professor T.H. Huxley and, through his mother, great-grandson of Dr Arnold of Rugby. Julian Huxley is his brother, Matthew Arnold was his great-uncle, Mrs Humphrey Ward his aunt. . . . Aldous once referred to his social background as "that impecunious but dignified section of the upper-middle class which is in the habit of putting on dress clothes to eat—with the most studied decorum and out of porcelain and burnished silver—a dinner of dishwater and codfish, mock duck and cabbage."

John Atkins, "Eton to the Mohave," in *Aldous Huxley: A Literary Study*, rev. ed., London, UK: The Orion Press, 1967, pp. 12–38. Copyright © John Atkins 1956, 1957, 1967.

Good-Spirited in Adversity

Ideas of impecuniosity [poverty] vary considerably. Young Aldous was sent to Eton and graduated to Balliol. For a little while he maintained family tradition (especially Arnold tradition) by teaching at Eton. But, like Gumbril Junior [Theodore Gumbril Junior, a character in Huxley's novel *Antic Hay*], he didn't stick it long. There are hardly any references to his own schooling in his writings, although there are boarding-school passages in *Eyeless in Gaza*. We know, however, that Dick Greenow [a character in Huxley's "The Farcical History of Richard Greenow"] considered the most precious gift of Aesop College, for those who knew how to use it, was "ample leisure". . . . This sounds like Eton.

Frank Swinnerton said Aldous was the tallest English author he had ever met. When he lived in Hampstead little boys used to call out to him, "Cole up there, guv'nor?" just as they did to Gumbril when he became the Complete Man. This, in conjunction with his long intellectual, bespectacled features, gave people the impression of hauteur. Expecting conscious superiority in him they naturally found it and accused him of an excessively lofty manner. In fact, he loved conversation and was usually full of high spirits. He revelled in long words but not because they were long—they came naturally to him. Swinnerton noted the constant use of the words "fantastic" and "incredible" in Huxley's conversation, particularly his narrative. He seemed to have an enviable knack of meeting odd people and seeing odd sights.

With his great gifts he found entrance to the literary world comparatively easy. He contributed to *Wheels*, the Sitwell [siblings Edith, Osbert, and Sacheverell] rival to *Georgian Poetry*, published his own volume of verse, *The Burning Wheel*, in 1916 and was one of the editors of *Oxford Poetry* in 1917. He contributed essays under the pseudonym Autolycus to *The Athenaeum* under Middleton Murry's editorship, and some of these appeared in his first volume of essays, *On The Margin*.

In those days he kept good literary company. In the first number of *Art and Letters*, for instance, we find him alongside Richard Aldington, Siegfried Sassoon, Wyndham Lewis and [Henri] Gaudier-Brezska. In 1917, at a poetry reading organised on behalf of charity, with Edmund Gosse in the chair, he read with Robert Graves, Siegfried Sassoon and the Sitwells. He used to attend [Walter] Sickert's breakfast parties with Nina Hamnett and W.H. Davies, Sitwell dinners with [Christopher] Nevinson and Roger Fry, and listen to Violet Gordon Woodhouse playing the clavichord with [T.S.] Eliot, Arthur Waley, Graves and Sassoon. In January 1920 we read of him attending the Olympia Victory Circus with Arnold Bennett, whom he watched drive off in a brougham-full of balloons. By this time Aldous was married to Maria Nys.

In *Laughter in the Next Room* Sir Osbert Sitwell gives a characteristic portrait of Aldous visiting him in hospital just after the war. He looked "interestedly disinterested, aloof," and was a study of Nonchalance in trousers. He could already talk fluently about everything under the sun, particularly modern theories of science, politics, painting, literature and psychology, but—what was peculiarly Huxleyan—at the same time did not despise the ordinary gossip of the day, although he treated it as a philosopher, with detachment and an utter want of prejudice.

> But he preferred to discourse of more erudite and impersonal scandals, such as the incestuous mating of melons, the elaborate love-making of lepidoptera [butterflies], or the curious amorous habits of cuttle-fish. He would speak with obvious enjoyment, in a voice of great charm, unhurried, clear without being loud, and utterly indifferent to any sensation he was making. Thus the most surprising statements would hover languidly in air heavy with hospital disinfectants. "From his novel conduct", I remember his announcing on one occasion, one must assume that Every Octopus has read [Roman poet] Ovid on Love.

And then, having made his point, Aldous would fall to silence again, "drooping into a trance-like state of meditation."

He wanted to be a doctor, yet became a sub-editor on *Vogue*. This in itself reflects the post-war dilettantism of the period, and is in turn reflected in his earlier work: observations on fashion-plates (as in "The Bookshop", *Limbo*), the essay on "Beauty in 1920" (*On The Margin*) and his close attention to women's clothes, evident in most of the stories and novels. But it was part of his comprehensive approach to his environment, his refusal to treat anything as being beneath his notice.

Yet it was certainly not a leaning towards the fashionable life that frustrated his desire to be a doctor. At the age of sixteen he had a violent attack of an eye disease called *keratitis punctata*, which seemed likely to destroy any possibility of an active career. For eighteen months he was nearly blind, and had to depend on Braille for reading and a guide for walking. Even when the condition had improved he was left with one eye just capable of light perception and the other with enough vision to permit him to read the two-hundred foot letter on the Snellen Chart at ten feet. At first he read with the aid of a magnifying glass, then was promoted to spectacles. But at the best he suffered from continual strain and fatigue, and was sometimes overcome by a sense of complete physical and mental exhaustion.

We get some idea of his courage when we realise that all the early work was written against this background of physical difficulty and spiritual depression. The high spirits seem the more remarkable, the moods of pessimism the more forgivable. Yet there are no direct references to his condition, save for a few in a light and bantering vein, certainly no traces of self-pity. The only occasions on which his private sorrow obtruded, and then not at all starkly, were in some of his poems, written as a young man when the disaster was fresh and appeared irredeemable. For instance, in "The Cicadas":

I hear them sing, who in the double night

Of clouds and branches fancied that I went

Through my own spirit's dark discourage-
ment,

Deprived of inward as of outward sight:

Who, seeking, even as here in the wild
wood,

A lamp to beckon through my tangled fate,

Found only darkness and, disconsolate,

Mourned the lost purpose and the vanished
good.

But, for the rest, he was matter-of-fact, even cheerful. When he went on his travels he tells us he always carried a plentiful supply of "optical glass". A pair of spectacles for reading, a pair for long range and a couple of monocles in reserve went with him everywhere. But in addition he carried three pairs of coloured glasses—two of lighter and darker shades of green, and one black. By these means he tempered the illumination of the world to his exact requirements. Sometimes he even felt thankful for his deficiency, for at a distance of more than four or five yards he was "blissfully unaware of the full horror of the average human countenance". Yet these countenances were clearly and often cruelly delineated in the novels.

In 1939 not even his greatly strengthened glasses were sufficient. Reading became increasingly difficult and fatiguing, and it became obvious that his sight was rapidly failing. It was then that he heard of the Bates method of visual re-education and of a teacher who had had several successes with the method. He decided to take the plunge. Within two months he was reading without spectacles and without strain or fatigue. Today [1956], although his vision is far from normal, it is about twice as good as it was when he wore spectacles. By this time he was in California and found that the strong and constant sunlight was an important factor in his recovery. Out of gratitude, and perhaps wonder and a desire to help others who had suffered from the same disability as himself; he took time off from fiction and *belles lettres* [literary works valued for their aesthetic qualities] and biography to write *The Art of Seeing*.

Theme of the Artificiality of Life

But I have gone too far ahead. Long before Huxley gained relief from his eye-strain he was astonishing, delighting and (in some cases) shocking the reading public with his early novels, *Crome Yellow, Antic Hay* and *Those Barren Leaves*. The War to End War [World War I] was over, the Bright Young Things had emerged, sex was blowing its lid off, discipline was being regarded as an offence against humanity, and the middle-class was becoming a collective laughing-stock for the emancipated. It was natural that, at the time, Huxley should have been compared with two other rebels, Noel Coward and Richard Aldington. All three chose as their target what Coward called the "massed illiteracy" of the now socially dominant bourgeois. . . .

Like most intelligent young men, who have imbibed more knowledge than they can effectively digest, Huxley believed he had a systematised grasp of life; in a few words, it was meaningless. If you cared to treat anything as important or significant, it was something you selected arbitrarily. But it was Huxley's merit that, on encountering facts and situations that could not be dismissed quite so lightly, he at first stretched his system to accommodate them and then abandoned it altogether. One of the first discoveries of this nature that he made was that pain, however ludicrous it may appear to the spectator, is always real. The person may be laughable, but his pain is as hard to bear as yours or mine. He expressed this troublesome conviction several times, but mainly in the lesser-known stories, and it has always remained with him. . . .

Huxley Travelled Extensively

It has often been remarked that the bohemianism of the post-war era was really a new form of provincialism. The province may have extended, geographically, to France and Italy, but emotionally it was no less narrow than suburbia. One of the first signs that Huxley was breaking out of it is to be found in the record of his journey round the world in *Jesting Pilate*. Before that he had travelled extensively on the continent, but his itinerary tended to be from art gallery to museum—and when he was not in an art gallery he was discussing it. For a time he admits, travelling was a vice, like reading. He read "promiscuously, omnivorously and without purpose." Later he realised that reading can easily become an addiction, like cigarette smoking. And at this period he was able to indulge both vices simultaneously. His brother Julian told Swinnerton that he had a special packing-case made for his *Encyclopaedia Britannica* when setting out on his journey to the Far East and America. On shorter journeys he was content to carry one volume only—any of the thirty-two would do. "It takes up very little room (eight and a half inches by six and a half by one is not excessive), it contains about a thousand pages and an almost countless number of curious and improbable facts. It can be dipped into anywhere, its component chapters are complete in themselves and not too long." The absorption of "curious and improbable facts" was possibly the only purpose in Huxley's life at this stage, before his conscience was aroused.

Most of his continental travels were done in a ten horsepower Citroën. He became a motoring fanatic. All was grist to his mill. In addition to the art galleries and encyclopaedia he pored over motoring papers, studying the news from the racing tracks and coming to terms with a new technology. Nothing was beneath his interest. And after all, technology was applied science. Unlike so many of his literary contemporaries he did not despise science. . . .

In fact, if he could have been born again and could have chosen his vocation, he would have been a scientist—"not accidentally but by nature, inevitably a man of science." He would rather have been [Michael] Faraday than [William] Shakespeare, despite the latter's posthumous reputation. His reasons for this choice are extremely significant; the scientist works in a non-human world, his work is not concerned with personal relationships and emotional reactions. "We are all subdued to what we work in; and I personally would rather be subdued to intellectual contemplation than to emotion, would rather use my soul professionally for knowing than for feeling". A secondary reason for this choice was that the scientist enjoyed much smaller social prestige than the artist and was therefore more immune from the intrusion of frivolous bores! . . .

America's Spiritual Emptiness

During this period one gets the impression that Huxley realised perfectly well the shallowness of the social round yet could not resist the temptation to participate. Although he knew it was a waste of time there was always the fear that, on just this one occasion, he might be missing something. He was ruefully aware that his objection to parties, fornication and idle chatter were only theoretical. In "The Monocle" (*Two or Three Graces*) Gregory asks himself why he still goes to parties, after so many disappointments—but he still goes. On the way to India Huxley was assured that he would have a "very good time" there. He knew what that meant: races bridge, cocktails, dancing till four in the morning, talking about nothing. "And meanwhile the beautiful, the incredible world in which we live awaits our exploration, and life is short, and time flows stanchlessly, like blood from a mortal wound. And there is all knowledge, all art" (*Jesting Pilate*). A frequently quoted proverb in Huxley's writing is *Video meliora proboque; deteriora sequor.* I know what I ought to do, but continue to do what I know I oughtn't to do. . . .

It was Huxley's first visit to America that finally impressed on him the imbecility of the search after a "good time". This was before the slump [the Great Depression], when American society as a whole was intent on the search, and genuinely believed that it had discovered the Grail. But Huxley was horrified. He realised instinctively that the spiritual emptiness would have to be paid for. (That you can never get anything for nothing has become one of his firmest convictions.) The moral conscience had been abolished and "amuse yourself" had become the sole categorical imperative. "The theories of Freud were received in intellectual circles with acclaim; to explain every higher activity of the human mind in terms of incest and coprophily [interest in excrement] came to be regarded not only as truly scientific, but also as somehow virile and courageous. Freudism became the *realpolitik* [politics focusing on actual power, not morals or principles] of psychology and philosophy. Those who denied values felt themselves to be rather heroic; instinctively they were appealing to the standards which they were trying, intellectually, to destroy" (*Jesting Pilate*). On his first contact with Californian society he was immediately reminded of [François] Rabelais [Rabelais wrote a series of five novels called *The Life of Gargantuan and Pantagruel*]: food in Gargantuan [tremendous in size] profusion, barbarous music throbbing unceasingly, flappers and young men wrestling amorously between each satiating course. But he knew something was lacking, a necessity of the Good Life that the Good Time did not provide. Rabelais would have missed the conversation and the learning, which serve as the accompaniment and justification of pleasure. In the Californian City of Dreadful Joy Pantagruel would soon have died of fatigue and boredom.

The world trip was a chastening experience. Besides the Good Time of California he had tasted the squalor and misery of the East. Soho and Mayfair fell into their true perspective, small and, on the world-scale, provincial. When he set out on his travels he had known all the answers: how men should live, how they should be governed, how educated and what they should believe. He returned without any of these "pleasing certainties". He discovered that his previous knowledge had been rather like that of the man who, asked how the electric light works, replied: "You just press the button". But he had acquired two important new convictions: that it takes all sorts to make a world, and that the established spiritual values are fundamentally correct and should be maintained. There was nothing new or breath-taking about these convictions, but "there is all the difference in the world between believing academically, with the intellect, and believing personally, intimately, with the whole living self".

In 1929 he wrote that whereas he would once have felt ashamed of not being up-to-date, he had now lost his fears. The goals of Modernity and Sophistication were bright but elusive. "I simply avoid most of the manifestations of that so-called 'life' which my contemporaries seem to be so unaccountably anxious to 'see'; I keep out of range of the 'art' they think it so vitally necessary to 'keep up with'; I flee from those 'good times', in the 'having' of which they are prepared to spend so lavishly of their energy and cash" ("Silence is Golden", *Do What You Will*). The youngest generation seemed to be interested in nothing outside its own psychology—but this he knew to be a dead end. Amusement, rather than money-making or power-seeking, consumed their energies. And how desperately bored they were! Among the lights, the alcohol, the hideous jazz noises and the incessant movement he felt a growing despondency overtaking him. By comparison with a night-club a church was positively gay [lighthearted]. Feelings and moods were justified by an appeal to the "right to happiness", the "right to self-expression". But it was a poor, insufficient rationalisation. Man became his own end. He was claiming to do what he liked, not because it was in harmony with some supposed absolute good but because it was good in itself.

Conduct, which Huxley had dealt with so airily in the early days, was now replacing aesthetics at the centre of his thought. In the relationship between man and the external world, something more realistic than the obscurantist egotism of Lucy Tantamount [a character in *Point Counter Point*] was required. He approached the problem in a brilliant essay entitled "Francis and Grigory" (*Do What You Will*). St. Francis was for him the supreme example of a man who subdued "things", including his own body and instincts, to his self. But Grigory Rasputin, despite his evil reputation, deserved credit for choosing the opposite rôle, the abasement of the spirit before the flesh, the will before the instinct, the intellect before the passions. It was a necessary correction to orthodox Christendom and contemporary Businessdom. In practice it might lead to the behaviour of a Tantamount, but it was not the product of despair and it did have a positive aim. Huxley liked to believe that Rasputin's self-indulgence was a means to an end, not an end in itself. In this re-orientation of his thought we can discern the influence of D.H. Lawrence, who had just died and with whom Huxley was on very intimate terms just before his death. The solution to the artist's (and others) quandary lay in the reconciliation of Francis and Grigory: subjugation of things to self and self to things.

This idea receives expression in three books of the middle period: *Point Counter Point, Do What You Will* and *Brief Candles. . . .*

A Mental and Artistic Crisis

Huxley was finding his way by a process of elimination. Examining himself, he discovered his personal graces and failings, set out to use to the fullest extent the capacities he had and to alleviate, if possible, the lack of those he had not. As a young man he enjoyed flux and change. In 1927 he could write that he felt no need of an Absolute which he regarded as "the introvert's subjective compensation for the multifariousness of strange and hostile objects" (*Proper Studies*). He had suggested the same thing in *Jesting Pilate* and in the following year he was to let Philip Quarles make a similar entry in his notebook (*Point Counter Point*).

The most faithful self-portrait of this middle period is in fact to be found in Quarles. His notebook gives us the current equivalent of a *Do What You Will* or *Proper Studies*. In one place he writes how much easier it is to know a lot about art and philosophy than about people. The real charm of the intellectual life lies in its easiness. "Living's much more difficult than Sanskrit or chemistry or economics." People try to drown their realisation of the difficulties of living properly in some kind of absorption: alcohol, fornication, dancing, movies, lectures, scientific hobbies—in his case, dilettantism. Under the heading Search for Truth it sounded noble and disinterested, but Quarles had discovered that the Search for Truth was just an amusement like any other—refined and elaborate, it is true, but still a substitute for living; and Truth-Searchers became just as silly, infantile and corrupt in their way as the boozers, the business men and the Good-Timers. The influence of Lawrence is again discernible; he had told Huxley that every man should be an artist in life, must create his own moral form. But the artist is in a peculiarly difficult position to follow this precept. He is compelled to cut himself off from society, to repress his "societal instinct", which Lawrence considered even stronger than the sex instinct. And familiarity with ideas, such as Huxley possessed, gave him and others the false notion that he understood all about personal relationships, because he was an "excellent psychologist". What he was beginning to discover was that he was only at home with *ideas* about personal relationships.

Obviously Huxley was passing through a mental crisis. The author of *Antic Hay* was dead—or morally transformed. A more realistic attitude was struggling to be born, but the struggle was a long one and, from about 1930 to 1936, it made only occasional appearances in his work. For the struggle was with himself, and this familiar phrase possessed for him more than its normal everyday meaning. He was literally seeking for his self, trying to uncover it from the mass of attitudes and ideas that he had previously mistaken for his interior essence. There is little reflection of what was going on in the work of the early thirties. *Brave New World*, for instance, still represented the intelligence turned outward. The great step forward was taken when he realised, not merely intellectually but through his own participation in the life of his time, that there was no real gulf between the inner man and the outer world, his internal psychology and his external actions. There must be some medium in which all moved, some principle which connected every aspect of a man's life. The multitudinous diversity of his past life, the flux and the change, were all appearances masking a reality that he felt impelled to discover. Then everything seemed to happen at once. *Eyeless in Gaza* (1936) indicated the way he had chosen, he became a pacifist (the inevitable outer response to the inner revelation), and in 1937 he cut loose from the familiar surroundings that had given birth to *Antic Hay* and *Two or Three Graces*, and went to live in the Mohave Desert. His choice was influenced by his wife's ill-health and by his own need for clear, strong sunlight.

Huxley Was Concerned with Political and Scientific Issues of the Day

Harold H. Watts

Harold H. Watts was a professor of English at Purdue University and the author of several books on literature, including Ezra Pound and "The Cantos".

Watts considers Aldous Huxley a man of strong conviction whose novels and essays deal with the search for values in twentieth-century civilization. Earlier works such as Crome Yellow *and* Antic Hay *use satire to point out the foibles in British society. In Huxley's later, more controversial works, such as* The Doors of Perception, *Watts proposes that Huxley advocates the use of hallucinogenic drugs as a way of heightening spiritual awareness.*

Aldous Huxley was born on July 26, 1894, at Godalming, Surrey. His parents were Leonard Huxley and [Julia] (Arnold) Huxley. Aldous Huxley was the youngest of three sons; Julian, the celebrated biologist, was his senior by seven years. (A middle brother, Trev, committed suicide in 1914.) Aldous Huxley's full christening name was Aldous Leonard Huxley; he early dropped the second name, which, it may be noted, was his father's name.

A Distinguished Ancestry

Future scholars may be able to determine whether the relation of Huxley to his parents was any model for the pattern of child-parent relationship which is rather normal in Huxley's fictions: one more marked by antagonism than respect and af-

Harold H. Watts, "Biographical," in *Aldous Huxley*, New York, NY: Twayne Publishers, 1969, pp. 15–27. Copyright © 1969 by Twayne Publishers, Inc. Reproduced by permission of Gale, a part of Cengage Learning.

fection. It is sufficient to note here that Huxley's parents were persons of much distinction in their own right. Leonard Huxley was educated as a Classics scholar and was, from 1901 onwards, editor of the *Cornhill Magazine*; he was also engaged in other literary tasks such as editions of the letters of T.H. Huxley, Jane Welsh Carlyle, and Elizabeth Barrett Browning. Mrs. Huxley was the founder of a girls' school. Her early death in 1908 was a shock, both deep and understandable, to her son; and the void she left was not successfully filled by Leonard Huxley's second wife.

Through his two parents, Huxley had a distinguished ancestry. His paternal grandfather, Thomas Henry Huxley, the champion of Charles Darwin and his theories, was a model of devotion to the pursuit of sober investigation wherever it led, and yet a stern moralist who could advocate the study of the Bible in the schools. Huxley's mother was a grand-niece of Matthew Arnold, also a kind of model of certain Victorian tendencies: concern with the discovery and cherishing of moral seriousness; concern—perhaps deeper than Thomas Henry Huxley's—with the implications for conduct of accumulating scientific insight. For Arnold had heard with dismay, on Dover beach, the retreat of the "sea of faith" that had supported and directed human consciousness for many centuries past; his somewhat prophetic insight allowed him to look forward to times when Classical studies and biblical piety would both have disappeared from English culture. (Through his mother, Huxley was also related to Mrs. Humphrey Ward, a novelist celebrated in her own day for sober treatments of questions disturbing the minds of her contemporaries.)

Viewing this combined inheritance, one is tempted to construct a neat paradigm to describe the two famous sons of Leonard and Julia Huxley: Julian worked out many of the implications of the confidence that his grandfather, Thomas Henry Huxley, had in the enlightenment that comes from scientific studies; and Aldous, intermittently sensitive to the dismay that came to his other ancestor, Matthew Arnold, was, in the latter portions of his career, determined to find substitutes for the healing that the "sea of faith" once offered mankind. But it is only just to note that Julian Huxley has labored outside the laboratory and has been as deeply concerned as his novelist brother for the good estate of man. Moreover, Aldous Huxley opened many a laboratory door at stages in his quest for surrogates to the ancient effects of the "sea of faith." The two brothers, whatever their theoretical differences—stemming chiefly from contrasting estimates of what man is—could join forces in their mature years in support of causes they mutually approved.

Schooling and Blindness

At the age of nine, Aldous Huxley was, like most English boys of his class, sent off to a preparatory school—to Hillside School, near Godalming. In the opinion of Huxley's cousin, Gervas Huxley, this school receives unflattering treatment in *Eyeless in Gaza* under the name of Bulstrode—a portrayal not entirely in accord with Gervas' own recollections of the years he had passed there with Aldous. Bulstrode, at least, is marked by snobbery and cruelty and overshadowed by the sexual troubles of young boys. That occasional rays of light fell into this darkness of Huxley's five years at Hillside is indicated by the recollections of others; for Huxley early impressed his peers with his intellectual superiority, and his pleasant vacations with his parents took him to the English lake country and to Switzerland.

After five years at Hillside, Huxley entered Eton (1908), where he endured troubling years. His mother's death was deeply disorienting for him; and, toward the end of his stay, occurred the onset of blindness—keratitis, or irritation of the cornea—that put an end to his hopes for a career in science. All the persons who recall Huxley's response to this challenge express admiration: Huxley taught himself Braille and praised the benefits of that skill for a boy who wished to continue to read after dormitory lights were extinguished. He also learned to type and composed a novel which he was never able to read because he lost the manuscript before the partial return of vision. An additional solace to him was his considerable ability on the piano.

From Eton, still in the company of his cousin Gervas, Huxley went to Balliol College at Oxford. In the course of his first year there, he had the happiness of recovering partial use of his sight although for many years he could read only with the aid of various sorts of glasses. (It was the wonder of later acquaintances that Huxley, handicapped as he was, was able to respond to so much in the works of art he constantly sought out.) Whatever his private troubles—concern with his sight, uneasiness over his inability, to share in the war experiences of his young relatives and friends—the Huxley of Oxford impressed others deeply as a young man confident in his emerging intellectual powers, always ready for elaborate discourse and sometimes for conversation, eager to take part in amateur theatricals, and pleased to contribute to the literary life of the University.

At this time Huxley already possessed the ready and curious erudition that—a frequent gibe—was drawn from the *Encyclopaedia Britannica* but certainly came from other sources as well. Later, in 1925, one of Huxley's preparations for a tour of the world was packing a set of the *Britannica* to travel with him. And a visitor to his household in the south of France in the 1930's recalls the presence of the *Britannica* on the shelves there. But Huxley's mind was more than encyclopedic; curious information was esteemed not for its own sake but for the uses to which it could be put. Huxley was also, by the time of his Oxford years, fluent in the French language; his later work is full of indications that he knew the byways as well as the main avenues of Gallic culture. There are also signs of ease with Latin, Italian, Spanish, and German.

During the years at Oxford, Huxley made his first appearances in print, although these had been anticipated at Hillside. His story "Eupompus Gave Splendor to Art by Number" appeared in a short-lived magazine, *The Palatine Review*; and a collection of poetry, *The Burning Wheel*, was published in 1916. Poetry, one should note, was a literary form that Huxley persisted in for the next ten years and then abandoned for fiction and essay—perhaps as a result of a discouraging suggestion from T.S. Eliot. In retrospect, Huxley continued to regard the writing of poetry as a normal activity of the gifted young; the seventeen-year-old Sebastian Barnach in *Time Must Have a Stop* (1945) composes verses—ones strongly resembling those of Huxley.

Huxley had already achieved the physical presence that everyone who knew him remarks on—tall, lean, and, perhaps because of his defect of vision, somewhat Olympian and detached in manner.

Near the end of his Oxford experience, Huxley made an acquaintance that was both defining and practically useful to a young man who wished to enter the literary world; he was introduced to Lady Ottoline Morrell, who presided over a casually assembled circle of the great and the promising at her manor house in Garsington, near Oxford. Lady Ottoline was the determined patroness of such figures as D.H. Lawrence, Lytton Strachey, Bertrand Russell, Katherine Mansfield, and John Middleton Murry; and Huxley easily won a place among these persons. The atmosphere of Garsington was that of free thinking and free speaking; the assemblage was one that was looked on with some suspicion because of its pacifist and other opinions, as the novelist Naomi Mitchison recalls—*she* was forbidden by her conventional parents to join it. Toward the end of World War I, Huxley joined other members of the group in agricultural labors which diminished his sense of uneasiness at being a non-combatant. But Garsington was important for him primarily because it gave him a view of the stimulating literary world which he hoped to enter; there is considerable agreement that Lady Ottoline's household was the model for the country house life that is represented in his first novel, *Crome Yellow* (1921). It was an atmosphere full of scorn for the smug and one that often cradled hopes for a freer, wiser use of human opportunity.

Upon completion of his studies at Oxford—from which he emerged with an Honors Degree in English literature—Huxley cast about for some means of support (he was already in love with a young Belgian refugee named Maria Nys, whom he had met at Garsington). His first attempt at self-support was teaching at Eton in 1918; at this task he was neither a notable success nor a great failure; he was provocative to some of his charges and an erudite enigma to others. Like Theodore Gumbril in *Antic Hay* (1923), Huxley retreated to London and soon found openings in literary journalism. He contributed reviews and articles to the *Athenaeum*, edited by John Middleton Murry; some of these, signed Autolycus in the journal, presently appeared as a first collection of essays, *On the Margin* (1923). Among his other labor was a stint as the dramatic critic of the *Westminster Gazette* in 1920 and 1921.

Marriage and Literary Reputation

Thanks to the degree of security he had attained, Huxley married Maria Nys in the summer of 1919. From this marriage one son, Matthew, was born. All accounts of the marriage, it is pleasant to note in contrast to the painful representations of love and marriage in much of Huxley's fiction, agree that it was a successful one. Mrs. Huxley, far from being a literary person herself, entered willingly into the activities of her husband; she shared in Huxley's lengthy travels; she typed his manuscripts and the manuscripts of his friends; she was a generous hostess in the various places in Italy, France, and California to which Huxley's wanderings led.

With the appearance of *Crome Yellow* (1921) and *Antic Hay* (1923), Huxley's reputation was quickly established. These novels, which struck readers as satiric and welcome rejection of the tedious past which their elders revered, enabled Huxley to abandon his journalism and to move away from the depressing climate of England to sunnier places, chiefly Italy and France in the 1920's and the early 1930's. It should be noted that Huxley's abandonment of formal journalistic employment in London did not amount to a halt of journalistic effort; the sheer bulk of his work—produced at the rate of about five hundred words a day, one observer relates—was occasioned by the necessity of meeting the modest needs of his own household and the sometimes less modest needs of the many persons Huxley was generous to.

By the middle of the 1920's, Huxley's life had achieved a pattern that lasted at least until 1937, when the Huxley's made their permanent settlement in California. During the 1920's Huxley's journeys through France, Italy, and Spain in a high-powered car and his trip around the world in 1925 and 1926 (recorded in *Jesting Pilate*) do indeed lack much of the passion that D.H. Lawrence was expending on his travels in the same period; Lawrence was forever discovering in ancient Etruscans or in modern Mexican groups a fashion of living that had been missed or lost in "civilized" England. In contrast, Huxley travels with the sense that there is much to learn and to be amused by, wherever one goes. For Huxley, there is almost no sense that one place of instruction—a distant country, a neglected era of the past—is necessarily a better place of instruction; it is certainly not likely to be the only one.

Instead, there is an eager and yet modest expectation that continues throughout Huxley's life: that a journey to Central America (recorded in *Beyond the Mexique Bay* [1934]) or to the Far East (*Adonis and the Alphabet* [1956]; American title: *Tomorrow and Tomorrow and Tomorrow*) will add pieces to the jigsaw on which an ingenious observer is working. One can observe that, even though Huxley lived for more than twenty-five years in southern California, the place was no more his home, in the conventional and perhaps sentimental sense, than some villa near Lucca [Italy] where he had halted for a short time in the late 1920's. California—like Lucca, or like some Hindu town visited only overnight—remained a place to be inspected, to be interpreted by ironic description and apt cultural parallels.

Friendship with D.H. Lawrence

During his years of chiefly Continental residence, Huxley wrote works that commanded—and command—wide public attention: *Point Counter Point* (1928), *Brave New World* (1932), and others. During his Italian sojourns in the late 1920's he formed his most celebrated friendship: the relation with D.H. Lawrence—that restless traveler who was a seeker for a locus of revelation rather than a cultural tourist like Huxley, who did not expect his travels to conduct him to a goal. Huxley had met Lawrence earlier and rejected Lawrence's suggestion of setting up an ideal colony in Florida. After 1926, however, and to the time of Lawrence's death in 1930 in Vence, [France,] Huxley and his wife devoted themselves to the well-being of Lawrence and Frieda, his wife, with singular, self-effacing piety. It was concern that one can see in Huxley's offer of a car to the Lawrences, in the support that Huxley gave Lawrence in the disputes about *Lady Chatterley's Lover*, and in the last weeks of Lawrence's life. A continuing concern for the reputation of his dead friend was responsible for an edition of Lawrence's letters which Huxley edited—a collection still basic to present-day Lawrence scholarship. This evidence, as well as the picture of Lawrence drawn in the figure of Rampion in *Point Counter Point*, suggests that Lawrence's focus of gesture and aspiration was immensely suggestive to Huxley.

But this focus came by degrees to count less for Huxley in the troubled 1930's. From Lawrence and Italy, one might say,

Huxley's curiosity moved on to other places, works of art, persons, social experiments, scientific discoveries, and even personal investigations of drugs (LSD) and of hypnotism. Here also were items that had a right to a place in the intellectual equation that Huxley was, to the very end of his life, adding to and hoping to balance.

The decade of the 1930's—concluded for most modern imaginations by the descent of the smoky curtain of World War II—was for Huxley, as the years advanced, a time of restless change of location, terminated only by his settling in southern California in 1937. To a *New York Times* reporter, Huxley explained: "I stopped there on, my way to India, and because of inertia and apathy remained." There were stronger motives: the beneficial effect of the bright light of the region on Huxley's vision and the accessibility of a center where the techniques of Dr. W.H. Bates helped Huxley to improve his eyesight. In addition to *Brave New World* (1932), this decade was marked by two novels, *Eyeless in Gaza* (1936) and *After Many a Summer Dies the Swan* (1939). Highly significant for Huxley's passage from amused detachment to deep, undisguised concern is the long essay or tract, *Ends and Means* (1937), the first of several frontal attacks on a time notoriously out of joint.

Altering circumstances in Huxley's life are outward signs of his changed estimate of a writer's function. Like the hero of *Eyeless in Gaza*, Anthony Beavis, Huxley overcame his repugnance to public speaking and spoke at rallies on behalf of the peace and internationalism that, in his judgment, the mass of men were blind to; he allied his efforts with those of Gerald Heard and the Reverend Dick Sheppard to curb the insanity that was preparing men for general slaughter. As he was to do for the rest of his life, he delivered public lectures of his own to publicize views that he felt were for the general good. He performed acts of deep beneficence, as when, along with his brother Julian, he intervened with the British government,

The family house of Aldous Huxley in London, England. © Coaster/Alamy.

which was about to pass regulations that would make it impossible for English citizens to rescue Jewish women by marrying them.

Embracing Social Responsibility

If one wishes an almost symbolic expression of the change noted here, one can observe that one of the deepest friendships Huxley formed after the death of Lawrence was with Gerald Heard, whom he met in 1931, worked with in public causes, and re-encountered when he took up residence in southern California. Heard was not, like Lawrence, a man who turned aside from social responsibility in the name of winning closer contact with blood or instinct or life-force. He was, instead, a man deeply attentive to the human uses of all the findings of science and sociology and psychology; in fact, his later development in California runs parallel to Huxley's own. It was in California that Heard had already encountered teachers of Eastern wisdom, the Vedanta; and, with another English expatriate, Christopher Isherwood, Heard had pursued the study of the wisdom of India. With this circle—formally known as the Vedanta Society of Southern California—Huxley associated himself.

With mutual encouragement and with the help of Hindu instructors like Krishnamurti and Swami Prabhavananda, the English writers labored to reconcile the West with the East in such works as Heard's *The Eternal Gospel* (1946) and as Huxley's *The Perennial Philosophy* (1945). The work of these English exiles has aroused irritation in many quarters; it is enough to observe at this point that Huxley was perhaps stimulated by Heard's insights and found a clue that sufficed him when the insights of D.H. Lawrence had lost their power to illuminate his mind. Was it a clue that betrayed Huxley's talent? This question must wait upon an inspection of the latter half of Huxley's work; it is not surprising that Christopher Isherwood judges that Huxley's best books were those of the second half of his life.

Shortly after his arrival in California, Huxley gave other signs of his amazing and, to some, disconcerting expertise. Aided by Anita Loos, the author of *Gentlemen Prefer Blondes*, Huxley had the opportunity of writing the film-script of *Pride and Prejudice* in 1941, a remarkably faithful treatment of Jane Austen's novel. (He was also involved in work on two later films: *Jane Eyre*; a treatment of the life of Madame Curie; and the film version of his successful play, *The Gioconda Smile*—which was given the more sensational title, *A Woman's Vengeance*.)

There is little sign that Huxley, in the last twenty-five years of his life, found reason to modify the harsh judgments that he had pronounced on West Coast civilization in *Jesting Pilate* (1926). He could express admiration for the deserts and mountains; he continued the interest in painting which he had taken up many years before in southern France; and he was particularly impressed by the Joshua trees of the California desert. He could also take pleasure in the wide variety of social contacts the Los Angeles area provided for him. (Anita Loos's account of a picnic at which the Huxleys, along with Miss Loos, Greta Garbo, the Hindu teacher Krishnamurti, and others were nearly arrested as vagrants by an angry policeman is an amusing record of the position of the arts in America and has a startling resemblance to incidents that Huxley invented for his fiction.) But Huxley found no reason to question his earlier estimate of the deleterious forms of materialism and pleasure-seeking that continued to be the norms of human action in his place of final residence. An observer has found as rather strange Huxley's indifference to the vulgarity of the furnishings of the house where he lived for many years. Perhaps Huxley's amused tolerance is not unlike that which the sophisticated person offers popular arts; to find them amusing rather than contemptible is proof of one's complex powers of insight.

Experimentation with Drugs

During the last ten years of life, Huxley aroused attention, some of it unfavorable, by the personal experiments he made, under the careful direction of his friend, Dr. Humphry Osmond, with hallucinogenic drugs; here Huxley found, as he makes clear in *The Doors of Perception* (1954), material aids to the intensification of insight that, supposedly, some of the great visionaries of the past had achieved by themselves. It is just to note that Huxley's interest in drugs, in hypnotism, and in some of the other fringe benefits of existence in California were not random; human reaction was, as Huxley judged the matter, pitiful in its narrowness of range, and the student who was concerned to broaden that range and to intensify its subtlety would investigate all the means that presented themselves.

These interests did not, however, cancel Huxley's concern with the immediate problems which civilization faces. He continued the lecturing he had begun in the late 1930's; he accepted invitations to speak at universities and meetings devoted to such causes as control of hunger and excessive growth of population, and he contributed to schemata useful for the deliberations of international congresses. Like his brother Julian, Huxley was in his last years something of a public figure; various awards and citations underlined the degree of importance he had won.

All the recollections of Huxley's last decade underline the persistence of his kindness, his pursuit of useful information, and his stoic endurance of his own physical sufferings, including the cancer that finally brought about his death. Mrs. Huxley had died of the same disease in 1955. In the year following his wife's death, Huxley married again; his second wife was Laura Archera, an Italian concert violinist. All reports indicate Huxley's courage and resignation when a brush fire destroyed his home and all his papers in 1961; the cancellation of the material detritus of the past was, Huxley indicated, in a way beneficial: it cleared the way to new tasks. This attitude, less strikingly, marks most of Huxley's work: in many books he gives the impression of taking up problems for the first time rather than, as a matter of fact, for the fourth or fifth time.

Huxley's death took place on November 22, 1963—the same day as the assassination of President John Kennedy. The progressive effects of cancer had been working for three years; they had scarcely diminished Huxley's flow of composition and even his continuing travel; and, in the last week of his life, he managed to finish an essay entitled "Shakespeare and Religion."

Such are the outlines of Huxley's life: outlines it is useful to refer to, from time to time, as one undertakes an analysis of his work, various and abundant. It should be clear that there is little of the shocking or the *outré* in his personal behavior or relationships; intellectual boldness and its reflection in prose and spoken argument were, for Huxley, a sufficient repudiation of elements in the past that deformed the present.

Huxley's Vision Changed from Materialism to Mysticism

Orville Prescott

Orville Prescott was the book critic of the New York Times *for twenty-four years. He is also the author of* In My Opinion, *a book of literary criticism;* The Five-Dollar Gold Piece, *an autobiography; and two books on the Italian Renaissance.*

In this obituary Prescott calls Aldous Huxley one of the most brilliant and versatile of twentieth-century writers. Prescott finds Huxley unusual among authors because he changed his worldview during the course of his career. He began his career as a skeptical materialist and ended it as a spiritual mystic. Prescott asserts that the one element uniting Huxley's works is his didacticism—all of his works are vehicles for his political and social views.

The death of Aldous Huxley removes from the world of letters one of the most brilliant, learned and versatile of 20th-century writers.

His reputation had reached its peak with the publication of *Brave New World* in 1932. That blistering satire of a future civilization dedicated to comfort, sexual indulgence and complete control of the individual by the state was the predecessor of many later political satires, none of them as clever or as abrasive.

Unlike most writers, whose basic point of view remains unchanged, Mr. Huxley was a skeptical materialist when he wrote the brilliantly clever novels that made him famous, notably *Those Barren Leaves* and *Point Counter Point*, and a mys-

Orville Prescott, "Two Aldous Huxleys," *The New York Times*, November 24, 1963, p. 22. Copyright © 1963 by The New York Times Company. Copyright renewed 1991 by The New York Times Company. Reproduced by permission.

tic of a private sort during the last 30 years of his life. Mr. Huxley's mysticism was expressed in biographies, histories and fiction and seemed to many readers to be a combination of Oriental, Christian and personal elements.

Always Didactic

But whether he was writing the satirical comedies of his youth or the less artistically effective novels of his maturity Mr. Huxley was always a didactic creature even when he had no proper pulpit from which to denounce or to exhort. His learned, savage and eloquent discourses usually overburdened his fiction to a dangerous degree. Few modern writers have been more earnest, more learned in art, literature, history and science; but quite a few have written novels much superior to his as creative works of art.

The trouble was that Mr. Huxley was not really at heart a story teller. Satire was a medium he felt to be his own. In the nineteen-twenties and early thirties he used it to express the scientific materialism, postwar disillusionment, hedonism and moral cynicism that were then fashionable among many intellectuals.

The characters in his early novels acknowledged no obligation and lived by no standards save their own tastes and whims, their own greed and lust. At first Mr. Huxley enjoyed their company. He appreciated their charm and wit. But in successive volumes he became more and more disgusted with his parasitic people. Finally, he reached a state of rage where he was skinning his characters alive and rubbing salt in their wounds.

Huxley Saw His Own Vision

But moral outrage without moral conviction was impossible for him to sustain long. Horrified by the cruelty and suffering of the Fascist wars and by the Communist and Nazi cults of the totalitarian state, Mr. Huxley seemed to see his own vision on his own Damascus road and thereafter to find refuge in his own interpretation of mystic experience.

Readers who enjoyed the satirical comedies did not necessarily take to the mystical books. Readers who might have understood and admired Mr. Huxley's mysticism did not always appreciate the urbane prose in which it was expressed; were sometimes repelled by Mr. Huxley's recondite references. The result was that Aldous Huxley was more popular, more critically admired and more imitated by younger writers in the twenties and thirties than he ever was afterward.

Social Issues in Literature

CHAPTER 2

Brave New World and Bioethics

Brave New World Is Concerned with Government's Controlling Citizens Through Science

Sybille Bedford

Sybille Bedford was a German-born English writer who wrote the authorized biography of Aldous Huxley. As a teenager Bedford lived in the same small fishing village in France as Huxley and his wife, Maria. The Huxleys arranged a marriage of convenience with an English army officer for Bedford, who had Jewish ancestry, to prevent her possible deportation to a Nazi concentration camp. Bedford is the author of A Legacy: A Novel.

In the following selection, Bedford explains that Huxley began writing Brave New World *to satirize the works of H.G. Wells, but as he wrote it, it began to take on a more serious purpose. Huxley's theme is not the progress of science, or what science will do in the very distant future. Rather, Bedford maintains that he is concerned with what will be possible very soon. In* Brave New World *Huxley warns that it will be technologically possible for government to manipulate citizens through genetics, unless society is very careful to avoid it.*

In Sanary, in April, Aldous began to write his Bad Utopia. He wrote it in four months. It all began light-heartedly enough. It was time to produce some full-length fiction—he still felt like holding back from another straight novel—juggling in fiction form with the scientific possibilities of the future might be a new line. Twenty-five years after, an American

Sybille Bedford, *Aldous Huxley: A Biography*, New York, NY: Alfred A. Knopf, 1975, pp. 240–46. Copyright © 1973, 1974 by Sybille Bedford. Reproduced by permission of Ivan Dee Inc. In the U.K. by permission of Lutyens & Rubinstein, agents for the author's estate and by Alfred A. Knopf, a division of Random House Inc.

acquaintance asked Aldous whether he had any idea that *Brave New World* would be considered prophetic, that it would be regarded as an influential philosophical work. "He replied with a kind of tender but self-deprecating affection for his own past that he had been having a little fun pulling the leg of H.G. Wells. At least it had started out that way until he got caught up in the excitement of his own ideas."

Wells' views on the effects of applied science were rosy; Aldous had his doubts. Take eugenics for instance—the increase, by deliberate breeding, of some of the inheritable qualities such as intelligence and ability. An intrinsically desirable change, you might say, but would it have desirable results? What would happen to a society compelled by law to breed exclusively from its most gifted and successful members? Four years earlier already, Aldous had had this to say on the subject.

> . . . It is obvious that all the superior individuals of the eugenic states will not be permitted to make full use of their powers, for the good reason that no society provides openings for more than a limited number of superior people. No more than a few can govern, do scientific research, practise the arts . . . or lead their fellows. But if . . . every individual is capable of playing the superior part, who will consent to do the dirty work and obey? The inhabitants of one of Mr Wells's numerous Utopias solve the problem by ruling and being ruled, doing high-brow and low-brow work in turns. While Jones plays the piano, Smith spreads the manure. At the end of the shift, they change places; Jones trudges out to the dung-heap and Smith practises the A minor Etude of Chopin. An admirable state of affairs if it could be arranged . . .

"Personally," Aldous went on, "I find my faith too weak . . . The intellectually gifted are notorious for the ruthless way in which they cultivate their gifts."

"I'll tell you, Ed, this new technology is starting to really spook me out," cartoon by Dave Carpenter. CartoonStock.com. Copyright © Dave Carpenter. Reproduction rights obtainable from www.CartoonStock.com.

In Aldous's counter Utopia, then, human beings are deliberately bred inferior as well as superior; Gammas and Identical Epsilon Semi-Morons as well as Alpha-Pluses. The principle of mass production, as one of the World Managers explains, is at last applied to biology. The theme, the well-known theme of *Brave New World*, is the effect of science applied to human beings by their rulers at some approaching future point. (The theme was not the progress of science as *such*; Aldous's intention was not scientific prophecy, no foretelling of any probable specific technological development, such as if and when we might split the atom—bottled babies were just a serviceable extravagance—it was psychological prophecy.) The theme was that you could dominate people by social, educational and pharmaceutical arrangements:

> iron them into a kind of uniformity, if you were able to ma-nipulate their genetic background ... if you had a govern-ment sufficiently unscrupulous you could do these things without any doubt ...

And this, Aldous said in the London interview in 1961, "This *was* the whole idea of *Brave New World.*"

These things—projected forty years ago for the year 600 After Ford—were Pavlovian conditioning of children before and after birth, hypnopaedia, mind-changing drugs and pleasure-giving drugs, planned sexual promiscuity (". . . as po-litical and economic freedom diminishes, sexual freedom tends compensatingly to increase"), compulsory contraceptives, the prolongation of youth, euthanasia, total centralization of power, total government control and above all a foolproof sys-tem to standardize the human product. Today, we are still a longish cry from globally controlled production of human be-ings. Yet (as Aldous pointed out in 1961) "We are getting more and more into a position where these things *can* be achieved.

> And it's extremely important to realize this, and to take ev-ery possible precaution to see that they shall *not* be achieved. This, I take it was the message of the book—*This is possible: for heaven's sake be careful about it.*

Brave New World Is Concerned with the Misuse of Science for Power

Joseph Needham

Joseph Needham was a professor, biochemist, and sinologist who served as master of Gonville and Caius College at Cambridge University. He is the author of Chemical Embryology *and* Within the Four Seas: The Dialogue of East and West.

In the following review, Needham, a respected scientist, states that what makes Brave New World *so horrifying is that Aldous Huxley did not exaggerate his science. For instance, his prediction of the cloning of numerous people with the same genetic constitution from one egg is possible, as experiments in this field were taking place at the time the review was written. Needham contends that Huxley is warning of the potential for a totalitarian government to manipulate its citizens through biological engineering.*

Mr. Huxley's theme [in *Brave New World*], embellished though it is by every artifice of that ingenuity of which he is master, is primarily dual, one of its aspects being the power of autocratic dictatorship, and the other, the possibilities of this power when given the resources of a really advanced biological engineering. The book opens with a long description of a human embryo factory, where the eggs emitted by carefully tended ovaries are brought up in the way they should go by mass-production methods on an endless conveyor belt moving very slowly until at last the infants are 'decanted' one by one into a highly civilised world. The methods of education by continual suggestion and all the possibilities of conditional reflexes are brilliantly described, and we are shown a world where art and religion no longer exist, but in which an *absolutely* stable form of society has been achieved, firstly, by sorting out the eggs into groups of known inherited characteristics and then setting each group, when adult, to do the work for which it is fitted, and secondly by allowing 'unlimited copulation' (sterile, of course) and unlimited sexual gratification of every kind. Here Mr. Huxley, whether consciously or not, has incorporated the views of many psychologists, e.g. Dr. [Roger] Money-Kyrle. In an extremely interesting paper ["A Psychologist's Utopia," 1931] Dr. Kyrle has suggested that social discontent, which has always been the driving force in social change, is a manifestation of the Oedipus complexes of the members of society, and cannot be removed by economic means. With decrease of sexual taboos, these psychologists suggest, there would be a decrease of frustration and hence of that aggression which finds its outlet in religion, socialism, or more violent forms of demand for social change. This doctrine is indeed an extremely plausible one, and provides an answer to the question of what the 'born' reformer is to do when the ideal communist state, for instance, has been brought into being. Supposing that we have what we regard as an ideal state, how shall we ensure its continuance? Only, says Dr. Kyrle, by removing the sexual taboos which make the 'born' reformer. Accordingly, Mr. Huxley shows us the state of affairs when the attack on post- and premarital, and pre-pubertal taboos has long succeeded. The erotic play of children is encouraged, universal sexual relations are the rule, and indeed any sign of the beginning of a more deep and lasting affection is rebuked and stamped out, as being anti-social.

Accurate Scientific Predictions

But Mr. Huxley, of course, sees so clearly what the psychologists do not see, that such a world must give up not only war, but also spiritual conflicts of any kind, not only superstition, but also religion, not only literary criticism but also great creative art of whatever kind, not only economic chaos, but also all the beauty of the old traditional things, not only the hard and ugly parts of ethics, but the tender and beautiful parts too. And it may well be that only biologists and philosophers will really appreciate the full force of Mr. Huxley's remarkable book. For of course in the world at large, those persons, and there will be many, who do not approve of his 'utopia', will say, we can't believe all this, the biology is all wrong, it couldn't happen. Unfortunately, what gives the biologist a sardonic smile as he reads it, is the fact that *the biology is perfectly right*, and Mr. Huxley has included nothing in his book but what might be regarded as legitimate extrapolations from knowledge and power that we already have. Successful experiments are even now being made in the cultivation of embryos of small mammals in vitro, and one of the most horrible of Mr. Huxley's predictions, the production of numerous low-grade workers of precisely identical genetic constitution from one egg, is perfectly possible. Armadillos, parasitic insects, and even sea-urchins, if treated in the right way, do it now, and it is only a matter of time before it will be done with mammalian eggs. Many of us admit that as we walk along the street we dislike nine faces out of ten, but suppose that one of the nine were repeated sixty times. Of course, the inhabitants of Mr. Huxley's utopia were used to it.

Huxley Also Got His Philosophy Right

And it is just the same in the philosophical realm. We see already among us the tendencies which only require reasonable extrapolation to lead to Brave New World. Publicism, represented in its academic form by Mr. [Ludwig] Wittgenstein

[Austrian-British philosopher] and Prof. [Moritz] Schlick [German philosopher] and in its more popular form by Prof. [Lancelot] Hogben [British scientist] and Mr. Sewell, urges that the concept of reality must be replaced by the concept of communicability. Now it is only in science that perfect communicability is attainable, and in other words, all that we can profitably say is, in the last resort, scientific propositions clarified by mathematical logic. To the realm of the Unspeakable, therefore, belong Ethics, Religion, Art, Artistic Criticism, and many other things. This point of view has a certain attraction and possesses, or can be made to possess, considerable plausibility, but in the end it has the effect of driving out Reason from the private incommunicable worlds of non-scientific experience. We are left with science as the only substratum for Reason, but what is worse, Philosophy or Metaphysics too is relegated to the realm of the Unspeakable, so that Science, which began as a special form of Philosophy, and which only retains its intellectually beneficial character if it retains its status as a special form of Philosophy, becomes nothing more nor less than the Mythology accompanying a Technique. And what will happen to the world in consequence is seen with perfect clearness both by Mr. Aldous Huxley and by Mr. Bertrand Russell. 'The scientific society in its pure form' says Mr. Russell, 'is incompatible with the pursuit of truth, with love, with art, with spontaneous delight, with every ideal that men have hitherto cherished, save only possibly ascetic renunciation. It is not knowledge that is the source of these dangers. Knowledge is good and ignorance is evil; to this principle the lover of the world can admit no exception. Nor is it power in and for itself that is the source of danger. What is dangerous is power wielded for the sake of power, not power wielded for the sake of genuine good.'

Such considerations, of course, do not solve the problem, they only convince us that a problem exists. But Mr. Huxley's orchid-garden is itself an exemplification of the contention that knowledge is always good, for had it not been for his imaginative power, we should not have seen so clearly what lies at the far end of certain inviting paths. To his convincing searchlight, humanity (it is not too much to say) will always owe great debt, and it must be our part to get his book read by any of our friends who suppose that science alone can be the saviour of the world.

Huxley Saw Power for Both Good and Evil in Science

Jenni Calder

Jenni Calder is the author of numerous books on literary and historical subjects, including Chronicles of Conscience: A Study of George Orwell and Arthur Koestler *and* The Enterprising Scot: Scottish Adventure and Achievement.

Although both George Orwell's Nineteen Eighty-Four *and Aldous Huxley's* Brave New World *share some characteristics as dystopian novels, Calder claims in the following selection that their differences in tone are attributable to the different times in which they were written. She finds their major substantive difference to be their attitudes toward science. Huxley was concerned about the potential for abuse of science in the hands of a cadre of highly trained scientists. Orwell was concerned about totalitarianism but did not see science as a contributing factor.*

The idea of utopia has always been a response to the current and the contemporary. Utopia is a way of dealing in the imagination with the problems of the present, although it may be formulated as solutions to the fundamental, perennial problems of men, women and society. Utopia, of course, suggests an ideal. Most of us would shrink from Huxley's vision of the future, all of us from Orwell's, but both of them provide solutions, they both in a sense solve major problems of their own times, although both at the expense of vital features of the quality of human life. They are rational solutions that demonstrate the inadequacy, in fact the horror, of rationality alone.

"Origins and Objects" by Jenni Calder from *Brave New World and Nineteen Eighty-Four*, pp. 7–16, © Jenni Calder, 1976, is reproduced by permission of PFD (www.pfd.co.uk) on behalf of Jenni Calder.

The Abuse of Power

Brave New World and [Orwell's] *Nineteen Eighty-Four* are usually placed in the category of anti-utopian fiction, nightmares not dreams, warnings not portraits of an ideal. Yet both authors were aware that there existed as they were writing processes of thought and action that could lead to what they described, and people who were more than ready to make human sacrifices in order to achieve progress or power. Progress and idealism have always attracted the human race. To be unable to believe that things can and will get better is at best negative, at worst destructive. But to believe that the realization of an ideal is worth any sacrifice, or that progress by its very nature *must* be good for humanity, is extremely dangerous. Orwell and Huxley were both very worried about the tendency towards these beliefs. . . .

That *Brave New World* and *Nineteen Eighty-Four* are very different in tone and atmosphere no one will contest. A major reason for their difference is, simply, when they were written. What draws them together is the concern the authors share for man and society, and similar reactions to certain specific features of society. . . .

Huxley Concerned with Overpopulation

Huxley felt increasingly that the problems of the world's immediate future would be those of overpopulation and starvation, of the environment and pollution. He was concerned with these issues long before they hit the headlines of public concern. But in the 1920s his worries were about the quality and the purpose of life. We can use his early novels as a guide to an understanding of the post–World War One generation of the privileged classes, their frustrations, their cynicism, their disillusion, their experimentation with different aims in life. Synthetic substitutes for loss of faith recur in his novels. They are peopled with characters who are experiencing post-war (and post-Victorian) disenchantment, to whom it seems only too clear they can no longer believe in the old ways of doing things, in the old social and moral structures, the old artistic conventions, but who are uncertain, in some cases tormented, about what to put in their place. Most of Huxley's characters are unhappy, even those who experiment with the synthetic with some gaiety. In *Brave New World* most of his characters are happy. They have been brainwashed into happiness, and whenever brainwashing cannot wholly work drugs can assist. The difficulties that face the characters in Huxley's contemporary novels have been eliminated, but what is the result? Along with indecision, suffering, human cruelty on a personal level, have been cast out creativity, independence, a sense of self. Individuality, the crux and centre of the human condition, has gone. Orwell's Oceania destroys it too.

In some respects the methods are not so dissimilar. While Huxley's sleeping babies absorb the whispers from tape recorders that determine their attitudes to themselves and others, the Oceanians are bombarded from microphones and telescreens. It is cruder, but essentially the same method. Both writers are reacting against the mindless persuasions of the advertising slogan, and Orwell specifically against the political catchword. Huxley identified advertising as one of the formative influences on modern life. Modern advertising had taken hold in the latter part of the nineteenth century, but it was in its first extravagant flowering in the 1920s. There is a memorable passage in [Huxley's] *Eyeless in Gaza* (1936) where the hero as a small boy is travelling in a train past advertisement boardings. His mood, his feelings, his whole life, seem to be symbolized by the vast and grotesque images he passes. Advertising was not only grotesque and vulgar, a cheapening of responses, it was dangerous, disturbingly powerful, a form of brainwashing. Orwell combines the grotesque and the dangerous in his giant posters of Big Brother that are such an inescapable feature of Airstrip One's drab townscape. In *Brave New World* there is no need for posters, for the work has been done in infancy by the whispering tapes.

73

Advertising was a direct expression of the capitalist, consumer society ethic and linked with the tyranny of the machine. Reaction against the ugly effects of industrialism was already well established. It was at the core of many of [John] Ruskin and [William] Morris's lectures and essays, and of the latter's *News From Nowhere* (1891). They were both writers who felt with all their being the devastations of industrial society. Right through Huxley's writings Henry Ford is a symbol both of the machine age and of conspicuous consumption and in *Brave New World* God has become 'Our Ford', money and the machine inexorably linked. Money is one of the problems that the new world has solved, for class is determined in the test tube and possessions are determined by class. There is no competition, no keeping up with the Joneses, no novelties to be grabbed for. The problem has been solved by rationalizing the status quo, confirming inequality in a cleanly scientific way. And it is in the area of science that the radical difference lies between Orwell's and Huxley's books. For Huxley was profoundly worried about the morality of science, about the fact that knowledge could mean power for evil as well as power for good, that science could destroy as well as discover, and about the fact that the more a small body of highly trained men found out about the way human beings function, the more easily could human beings be controlled. Perhaps his greatest fear was that the dangers could occur inadvertently, from the best intentions.

Orwell is worried about the power of totalitarian control, its methods and its effects, but not specifically about the responsibilities of science. The technology of Oceania is no more sophisticated than that which existed in 1948. In terms of science fiction it is crude. There has been no orientation towards making life easier, in fact many of the basic technological aids, lifts for instance, don't work. In Oceania all technological skill goes into the manufacture of armaments in order to perpetuate the state of war that is essential for Big

Brother to maintain power. Orwell sees the dangerous potential of science only in terms of overt power, not in terms of the kind of subtle influences in life that Huxley saw as the germs of the control of humanity in the future. Again, the explanation for the difference lies partly in the difference between 1930 and 1948. For Orwell in 1948 the overwhelming fact of existence was the terrible success of totalitarian power, which Hitler's defeat could not wipe out. For Huxley eighteen years earlier it was the lack of spiritual and moral values in a society shaken by its inability to cope with harsh realities and increasingly dominated by technology. The concerns of the two writers are similar, for the quality of life, for human decency, for creativity; it was their identification of the causes of the destruction of what they valued that was inevitably different.

Alarmed at Technological Progress

Both Orwell and Huxley regarded the word 'progress' with the greatest suspicion. For Huxley's generation, progress was a word that belonged with the Victorians, and indicated a belief in the inevitable improvement of humanity. Those who had lived through the First [World] War were profoundly sceptical about improvement. What did progress mean to ordinary men and women? How could exciting advances in the laboratory be measured against, for instance, the decline in living standards that post-war unemployment brought? How could the achievement of the dedicated scientist be measured against, for instance, his failure as husband and father, a favourite theme of Huxley's? There were very few who had a thought to spare for the social implications of technological advance, in spite of the fact that the nineteenth century had had a continual problem of the consequences of developing technology. For Orwell, progress could be symbolized negatively by the atom bomb; progress in technological terms meant destruction. Orwell's instincts led him to something like Morris's anti-machine utopia. He found modern technology profoundly distasteful, and revealed very little curiosity about scientific achievement—which always interested Huxley. But although he clearly knew less about what science was doing and could do than Huxley, Orwell shared the feelings of Huxley and many of that generation—he was only ten years younger than Huxley. He was young enough to view the Victorian and Edwardian periods with a nostalgia that Huxley could not share, but old enough to be profoundly affected by the First [World] War's shattering of traditional values. The comfortable faith of the Victorians in the interweaving of progress and Christianity backed by absolute moral values for the continuing improvement of all of mankind worth improving could not be recaptured.

Huxley Developed Spiritually

The destruction of belief operated differently on the two men. Huxley turned to a spiritual philosophy which he formulated in later books, and enhanced by his experimentation with drugs. Orwell believed socialism to be the answer; not the socialism propagandized by the theorists, but a socialism based on simple equality, community, and a radical relationship with work and the land. When he was in Spain during the Civil War he had a brief glimpse of what it might be like. It was one of the most important experiences of his life, and should be emphasized as an antidote to the pessimism of *Nineteen Eighty-Four*. Huxley also believed in community. He believed in people coming together, sharing their skills, diversifying their activities, co-operating in their responsibilities, and many of his ideas on these lines can be found in his last novel, *Island* (1962). To find Orwell's more optimistic and positive beliefs in the potential of mankind we must read his journalism and his essays. Too often, *Nineteen Eighty-Four* is read as his final testament. It should be remembered that he deliberately described the bleakest eventuality he could imagine because he so desperately did not want it to happen.

Nineteen Eighty-Four is a political book, and grew out of the political ideas and actions with which Orwell was familiar. *Brave New World* is presented as the logical development of a consumer and technology-orientated society, the means are scientific and the ends are self-perpetuation. It is not obviously political because Huxley foresees the withering away of politics. Once stability is achieved there is no need for politics. In 1946 he wrote a foreword to a new edition where he admitted that he had underestimated developments in atomic research and that the existence of the atomic bomb inevitably changed the shape of the future. The atom bomb (and he wrote this when Orwell was already planning his book) made Orwell's prognostication of a small number of totalitarian states in perpetual warfare a greater possibility. He also felt that developments since he wrote *Brave New World* brought the possibility of a technological utopia a great deal nearer than he had at first foreseen.

> Then, I projected it six hundred years into the future. Today, it seems quite possible that the horror may be upon us within a single century. That is, if we refrain from blowing ourselves to smithereens in the interval. Indeed, unless we choose to decentralize and to use applied science, not as the end to which human beings are to be made the means, but as the means to producing a race of free individuals, we have only two alternatives to choose from: either a number of national, militarized totalitarianisms, having as their root the terror of the atomic bomb and as their consequence the destruction of civilization (or, if the warfare is limited, the perpetuation of militarism); or else one supranational totalitarianism, called into existence by the social chaos resulting from rapid technological progress in general and the atom revolution in particular, and developing, under the need for efficiency and stability, into the welfare-tyranny of Utopia.

This is very close to what in fact Orwell wrote about *Nineteen Eighty-Four*. Fifteen years after *Brave New World* Huxley shares Orwell's feelings that the possibilities for the human race have narrowed. Satire was not the appropriate form for conveying the urgency that Orwell felt, although he had demonstrated his satiric skills a few years before in *Animal Farm* (1945) written during the War when Orwell still felt there was a chance for something like his kind of socialism. In 1931 there was human misery and political betrayal, there was weakness and muddle and hypocrisy, but there was no gargantuan threat. Satire was an appropriate form of exposure and attack. There were six hundred years in which to make sure there would be no brave new world. In 1948 time was running out, for Orwell himself and, he felt, for the human race.

Orwell's language bluntly conveys the possibility of disaster. One senses throughout the book a state of mind that had to dispense with frills and graciousness—although Orwell had always aimed for a style as direct and unadulterated as possible. One of the most impressive aspects of the book is the way in which the style is totally appropriate for the message. There is one moment, when the language can't quite do what is required of it, [the famous rats scene,] but the failure there arises from the choice of an inadequate symbol of the ultimate personal terror. Perhaps the greatest achievement of the book is the way in which Orwell has made language state so plainly, without strain or detectable exaggeration, so devastating a nightmare.

Huxley's touch is lighter. We can admire the sheer cleverness of the book, its cool wit, its finely prepared weapons. But the signs that *Brave New World* should never be read as merely a witty extravaganza are unavoidable. The book has an ugly climax for a very specific purpose. In eight years' time *Brave New World* will be more than half a century old and 1984 will have arrived. It is unlikely that 1984 will make *Nineteen Eighty-Four* irrelevant, or that *Brave New World* will become out of date in the foreseeable future.

Brave New World Warns of the Dangers of Consumerism, Genetic Engineering, and Technocracy

Robert S. Baker

Robert S. Baker (1916–2005) was a professor of English at the University of Wisconsin–Madison. His books include The Dark Historic Page: Social Satire and Historicism in the Novels of Aldous Huxley, 1921–1939.

Born into a family with a distinguished background in science, Aldous Huxley recognized the substantial contribution science had made to human progress, Baker suggests in the following selection. But he also understood the power of science and feared that in the hands of bureaucrats who valued power for its own sake, science could become perverted and used to control society. Baker contends that Huxley's greatest fear was the potential misuse of genetic engineering, but Brave New World *also reflects his warnings about the dangers of a society based on consumerism and ruled by technocrats.*

In a letter to E.M. Forster, written in 1935, only three years after the appearance of *Brave New World*, Huxley recorded a conversation with [Welsh mathematician and philosopher] Bertrand Russell in which Russell attempted to discern a ray of scientific light at the end of a historical tunnel darkened by the Great Depression, the rise of Adolf Hitler, and the increasing prospects of war in Europe and Asia: "Bertie Russell, whom I've just been lunching with, says one oughtn't to mind about

Robert S. Baker, "The Importance of the Work," in *"Brave New World": History, Science, and Dystopia*, Boston, MA: Twayne Publishers, 1990, pp. 7–10. Copyright © 1990 by G. K. Hall & Co. All rights reserved. Reproduced by permission of Gale, a part of Cengage Learning.

the superficial things like ideas, manners, politics, even wars—that the really important things, conditioned by scientific technique, go steadily on and up . . . in a straight, unundulating trajectory." Huxley observed that "it's nice to think so" but wondered "if that straight trajectory isn't aiming directly for some fantastic denial of humanity."

The Potential for Evil in Science

In *Brave New World* Huxley had already depicted one major form that such a denial of humanity could take and in doing so created an anti-utopian satire that has only gained in relevance over the intervening years. The reason for this lies with Huxley's decision to focus not simply on totalitarian politics in his vision of a future world state but specifically on the power impulse within science itself. Born into a family with traditional ties to science, Huxley respected scientists and regarded modern scientific methodology as one of the most significant achievements in human history. But he also viewed science, especially applied science or technology, as a powerful expression of darker forces as well as potentially enlightening ones. He feared that the combination of bureaucracy and technology would lead to the rise of a managerial class of technical specialists who valued order and security above all else. In short, he feared the rise of the technocrat and what [American social critic] Christopher Lasch has called "the shift from an authoritative to a therapeutic mode of social control." What especially fascinated him was genetic engineering and its potential capacity to completely transform human society, politics, and even the family.

What makes *Brave New World* such an unusually lasting work, still capable of addressing a contemporary audience with point and vigor, is at least in part attributable to Huxley's decision to concentrate on three interrelated themes: the rise of a society organized around mass consumption; the increasingly ominous developments in the field of genetics; and the political dangers posed—potentially—by the scientific special-

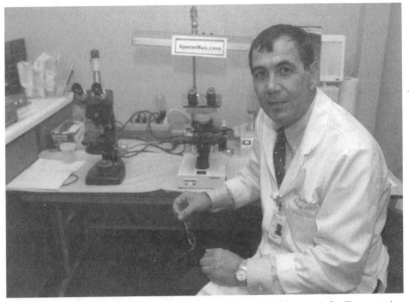

Dr. Panayiotis M. Zavos, an animal reproduction specialist and human infertility guru, is a member of an international team seeking to become the first to clone a human being. In Brave New World *Huxley explores the dangers of genetic engineering.* AP Images.

ist, particularly when organized and empowered by bureaucracy. The most menacing of these, as well as the most vividly and explicitly dramatized in *Brave New World*, is the complex mingling of benefit and political evil that Huxley saw in genetic engineering.

Moral Questions

Recently the National Academy of Sciences proposed a three billion dollar project to determine the complete chemical data base of human genes [the Human Genome Project, now completed]. Cattle have been cloned on Texas farms where patented genetically improved animals are regarded as the economic property of their "inventors." The ability to identify and locate the gene responsible for a particular inherited quality is no longer a scientific fantasy. The technique of cloning, that is, of creating virtually identical organisms by means of exchanging the nuclei of cells that contain genetic instructions, is a proven breeding method, while the Supreme Court of the United States has approved the making of genetically altered bacteria. The alteration of human beings, indeed the creation of genetically designed types for specific tasks, is a complicated moral and philosophical issue as well as a technical one. Most recently, British scientists have claimed to identify the gene responsible for schizophrenia. The idea that there is a direct link between a gene and complex behavior is no longer a highly speculative notion. The implications of this for our notions of individuality, free will, legal responsibility, and even racial and gender identity are only barely understood. Experimental advances in genetic engineering are outpacing our ability to prepare for their ethical and political consequences. If a gene is responsible for our sense of who and what we are, and if a gene can be altered or exchanged, then the personal attributes that compose our sense of irreducible selfhood can be radically modified, even obliterated. How do we utilize such awesome knowledge? Will we relinquish personal and legal autonomy? Who will be empowered by such knowledge?

Huxley's *Brave New World* is an attempt to trace out the darker lineaments of a science that promises a world of altered, cloned, and patented organisms. The problem for Huxley—and for us—is not genetics or science per se, but the potential exploitation of technological advances by a society given over to rampant consumerism, governed by massive centralized bureaucracy, and submissive to the ministrations of the expert or specialist. The twentieth century has seen so many scientific ideas appropriated by governmental bureaucracies for humanly and environmentally destructive purposes that it is hard not to assume that some bitter lessons may be in store for us once the genetic genie is out of the test tube.

A Study of Consumerism

Brave New World, however, is not reducible to a dark prophecy of the social implications of genetic research. It is also a study of a culture that has surrendered to mass consumption to the extent that its inhabitants are consumers, even commodities, but never citizens. It is a study of mass culture and industrial technology in a world state where economic and social stability compensates for the vulgarization of intellectual life and the absence of political responsibility. Its presiding feature is the dilution of high culture by means of mass media and popular entertainment. The infantile hedonism of its population and their cynical manipulation by a managerial elite is not as alien a vision as one might wish as the twentieth century draws to its close. Huxley's anti-utopia, then, is both a social and a political novel. The issues that it raises are as exigent and appropriate for 1989 as they were for 1932, perhaps even more so as a result of the even greater complexity of late twentieth century society and its extraordinary advances in technology.

Brave New World Reflects the Gender Bias of Its Time

June Deery

June Deery is associate professor of literature and media studies in the Department of Language, Literature, and Communication at Rensselaer Polytechnic Institute. She is the author of numerous works, including Aldous Huxley and the Mysticism of Science.

In the following selection Deery argues that there is a gender bias in the technology in Brave New World, *with females presented as inferior to males. In some cases, Deery states, Aldous Huxley is critical of this inequality—for instance, in the sexual interplay where women's physical characteristics are commented on by men as if they were horseflesh. In other instances, Huxley mirrors the gender bias of his time. To support this position, Deery points out that all the people in authority in* Brave New World *are male. Despite the fact that Huxley has imagined a different technological world, she contends, he has kept the same repressive gender politics.*

In *Brave New World*, which began as a parody of [H.G.] Wells's *Men Like Gods*, Huxley has a good deal of fun with technological innovations and anticipates several trends. Here technology underpins the whole of society and is worshiped in the name of [Henry] Ford. In detailing its various manifestations, Huxley approaches the technological fetishism of science fiction, yet there is not enough hard science for his accuracy to be tested. Fortunately, he has a happy knack for coining convincing terminology and at once giving it an air of familiarity. . . .

June Deery, "Technology and Gender in Aldous Huxley's Alternative(?) Worlds," *Extrapolation*, vol. 33, no. 3, Fall 1992, pp. 258–265, 271. Copyright © 1992 by The Kent State University Press. Reproduced by permission.

A Revolution in Psycho-Technology

Huxley anticipates everything from cloning, which only began with animals in the 1950's, to so-called test-tube babies, first successful in 1978, years after Huxley's death. The fact that Huxley's brother Julian and family friends such as the Haldanes were top biologists made Huxley privy to many current and anticipated developments. In turn, *Brave New World* spurred on research in certain fields, according to the testimony of some biologists. But the really big revolution, Huxley predicts, is not only in bio- but also psycho-technology, and here again he was ahead of his time.

The scientific attitude in the new world is rigidly Baconian [after English Elizabethan philosopher and scientist Francis Bacon]. Fordian researchers view themselves as conquistadors who, in an ecstasy of quantification, are out to put nature in its place. They delight because they have graduated from "the realm of mere slavish imitation of nature into the much more interesting world of human invention". All of this is of course regarded as appallingly hubristic [arrogant] by the author. Note how the process of growing the human fetus is described as dependent on "massive doses of hog's stomach extract and foetal foal's liver". And the idea of deliberately disabling a future human being, which is common practice on this production line, is surely repugnant, as is the sadistic postnatal conditioning with electric shocks, all in the Procrustian determination to fit the individual human being to the State's requirements.

But to what ends exactly? This is the question Huxley would have us append to every discussion of technological means. In this case the aim is simply to keep the machinery turning and maintain all citizens, male and female, in a state of calm though superficial contentment. Each has a limited and specialized function in the great mechanism of the State, the whole being lubricated by synthetic drugs. Any one individual knows very little about anything beyond his or her own specialized task. For example, Linda used to inject chemicals into test tubes, but when her son asks where chemicals come from she can only reply: "Well, I don't know. You get them out of bottles. And when the bottles are empty, you send up to the Chemical Store for more". Interestingly, in *Brave New World* even science has been replaced by technology. "Pure" research has been muzzled to create a permanent state of normal science where technologists deal only with immediate problems and none risk theoretical or metaphysical upsets. In accordance with Fordism, truth and beauty have been replaced by comfort and one brand of "happiness" for all, a happiness which to Huxley signals humanity's quiet and irreversible self-destruction.

Women Inferior in *Brave New World*

But how does technology impact on female experience in particular? In answering this, one uncovers a gender bias in Huxley's technocracy, though such a bias is nowhere explicitly stated as a founding principle. We quickly learn that classes are rigidly defined, but there is nothing to suggest that within each class women are to be regarded as inferior to men. In practice, however, after the 200 meter mark when sex is discovered, citizens appear to be treated differently according to gender, and the difference often means inequality, with women being assigned the lower status. In some instances, Huxley both recognizes the bias in the system and explicitly condemns it, but in other instances it is a function of his own perspective and he is oblivious to the inequalities his illustration introduces.

Interestingly, it is possible to argue that in some areas, despite its being a dystopia, *Brave New World* offers women a better deal than the contemporary British society of the 1930s. There is no housework, no wifely subjugation, no need to balance children and a career. And if women do not appear to have the vote (which in Britain they had gained only six years earlier), then neither do the men, for all are equally disfranchised in this society. Yet, for all this, if we compare their position to that of men in *Brave New World*, women are less well off. A dystopia is, of course, a negative picture, but this does not imply a simple reversal, when what appears to be approved is really condemned and vice versa. If women appear to have achieved a modicum of freedom, this is not frowned upon by the author, but then the disadvantages that they in particular face are not necessarily condemned either. The picture is much more complex. In fact, Huxley has often confused his readers because not everything in *Brave New World* is viewed as unpalatable. The point here being that one of the things Huxley does not always portray as objectionable is woman's relatively inferior role.

On occasion, he does recognize and explicitly criticize women's treatment in this society. This is most evident in his portrayal of sexual interplay. At first, the general promiscuity is seen as amusingly novel, and there is no serious discussion of what it reveals about a woman's position relative to men. The anonymous narrator is not explicitly gendered. Indeed, Huxley's desire to create a sense of lifeless uniformity means the language he employs is often less gendered than one might expect in a text of this period. Yet our first view of a woman is undoubtedly through male eyes, and the first comment is on her sexual attractiveness, or, from T.S. Eliot, her "pneumatic" appeal. We subsequently learn that the correct etiquette is for a man to pat a woman on the behind and murmur "charming" while she returns a deferential smile. This sort of behavior rapidly becomes less amusing when it is pointed out that in this society women are seen, and regard themselves, as "meat", and (as in our society) meat which must be lean, not fat. While chewing their sex-hormone gum (we don't see women using these stimulants), men compare different women as sexual partners and seem to strengthen their own bonding by recommending previous lovers. "'Yes, I really do advise you to try her,' Henry Foster was saying. . . . 'But, my dear chap, you're welcome, I assure you'". According to Huxley's description, men tend to ask women out on dates, and it is they who drive the helicopters (this, I think, is crucial). All of this may be because upper-class men appear to date lower-class women, a class difference which en-genders another hierarchy. But as to why this is so or how common it is, we are given no clue. What we do witness is that this pattern makes it difficult for the female to refuse her body to her higher-caste sexual partner. (For women, it seems, "free love" means always having to say yes). Thus Lenina, in love with someone else, has to dope herself before having sex with a highly-placed male, but we don't see a man prostituting himself in this fashion. Bernard, the misfit, finds this attitude towards women repugnant and expresses his distaste at the men's locker room conversation: "'Talking about her as though she were a bit of meat. Bernard ground his teeth. Have her here, have her there. Like mutton. Degrading her to so much mutton'". It is an attitude that is reinforced in the world of entertainment, if the film Huxley chooses to describe is anything to go by. This latest movie, or "feely," depicts a Beta blonde who, after being abducted by a lower-class black male, is rescued by a trio of upper-class white males and, in gratitude, becomes the mistress of all three of them, thus preserving both a gender and, it seems, racial hierarchy. Off the screen too, we note that the popularly admired type is the athletic, powerful, sociable "he-man" who always gets his girl. And it *is* always "he" who gets his "girl" in this hermetically heterosexual society.

Bias Reflects Huxley's Society

It may be that Huxley is deliberately using the movie to highlight these biases, and it may be that he generally depicts a higher-class male soliciting a lower-class female in order to disclose a gender inequality. Certainly there is some distaste for the view of women as sexual "meat," but it may also be, and I think this is more likely, that men propositioning women and men driving helicopters is merely an unthinking mirroring of Huxley's own society. There are occasions when one cannot be sure that Huxley recognizes or would have us recognize instances of sexual discrimination which appear embedded in the system; for example, as opposed to the "Girls' Dressing-Room" the men emerge from the upper-class "Alpha Changing Rooms". This might be interpreted as a revelation that this society regards men not only as superior but also as the norm. However, none of this reading is actually underscored in the text, and so we are at a loss to decide whether the bias is the dystopians' or Huxley's.

There are other instances of simple neglect. Thus, we can assume that numerous upper-class females exist somewhere in this society—there is nothing which precludes this—but in Huxley's account we get only a brief glance of one of them—the headmistress at Eton. Even here we encounter her when she is in a position of need relative to the AlphaPlus male who approaches her, and we note that her superior is a male Provost. The name of this upper-class female is, incidentally, "Miss" Keate, surely an anachronistic form of address in a society where there is no marriage. Perhaps Huxley has forgotten this in his desire to recreate the stereotype of the spinsterish headmistress, the woman who achieves position only by forfeiting her "true femininity."

In other cases it is even clearer that the gender bias is not, in fact, part of the dystopian system but is a function of Huxley's subsequent and unmindful portrayal of certain details once the society's basic principles have been established. Obviously there can be no denunciation where there isn't even a recognition of injustice. Rather, what we find is an automatic importation of the sexist norms of Huxley's own society into the imagined world. It is not a question of deliberately portraying the dystopia, "the bad place," as objectionable because, among other things, it treats women unfairly relative to men. Instead, the unequal treatment is frequently attributable to Huxley's own viewpoint. Rarely is the citizen in any dystopia in an enviable situation, but Huxley's portrayal goes further by placing women in an even lower position than men, *and* by not making a point of it. In short, there are many unattractive features of this society, but women's lack of position is not foregrounded as one of them.

Men Are in Power

Though there is nothing we know of in the dystopian constitution to bar them, Huxley simply fails to offer examples of women in power. The World Controller, the Director of Hatcheries and Conditioning, the Arch-Community Songster—all are men. There is even a male Assistant Director of Predestination (!), with the male gods of Ford and Freud hovering above. All of the women we encounter are slight characters, more objects than subjects, who are not able to break through the constraints of their society, much less Huxley's two-dimensional characterization, as some of the men begin to do. Although [Krishan] Kumar suggests that Lenina's falling in love might be the only door to overturning the present regime, it is such a static, one might almost say apolitical, society that it is difficult to see any possibility of upsetting the status quo to benefit either men or women.

Again, take the position, an important one in this society, of the technologist. The senior figures we encounter are invariably male. It is hardly surprising that, as recent studies have shown, there is a masculinist bias at the roots of modern science, both as an enterprise and worldview; what *Brave New World* does is simply reflect and perpetuate this tradition. We note that the novel opens with knowledge being handed on from senior males to younger male students. The association of technology with masculinity is reinforced by the fact that the sign for males in this society happens to be identical to the divine symbol of Fordian technology, the T. However, this identification is never explicitly remarked upon in the text and it is not clear if Huxley makes the association knowingly. Fertile women, on the other hand, are represented by a circle, which, apart from its obvious genital associations, suggests zero, nothingness, hollow space, and passivity. Moreover, if we see it as our own symbol of women (♀ Venus) minus the Christian cross, then, as men have gained divinity, women have had it taken from them. Other women who have been sterilized are designated by a question mark, as though suspicious or doubtful, and certainly something to snigger at. These "freemartins" do not constitute a third gender. They are still heterosexual and feminine, though, incidentally, since the latter comes from the root "to suckle," none of these childless women are in fact strictly "feminine." In any case, it is not clear if Huxley acknowledges a bias in the labeling of any of these categories (nor have I seen it outlined in any other critical works).

When it is a question of possessing knowledge or having an education, once again it is the men who appear to be in a superior position. In Huxley's account, women merely enter as narrative feeders, asking them for explanations. "'Why do the smoke-stacks have those things like balconies around them?' enquired Lenina. 'Phosphorous recovery,' explained Henry telegraphically", and he then goes on to lecture her at some length on this and other matters. Such interactions can again be explained by the fact that Huxley chooses to portray upper-class males addressing lower-class females. Instead of being scientists and leaders, the women we encounter perform auxiliary, service roles in nursing, teaching, secretarial and factory work—the sort of jobs their contemporaries were in fact given in Huxley's society. These women therefore don't do science; they have science done to them. One area where technology has fundamentally altered female experience is motherhood, or, to use the industrial metaphor, "reproduction." In *Brave New World*, complete ectogenesis, not just in vitro fertilization, is the norm, which means that the site of reproduction is no longer the female body.

No Power to Reproduce

Again, why is this done? The ostensible reason, as Huxley presents it, is that ectogenesis facilitates conditioning and the efficient production of future citizens. This much is true. But could it also be attributed to a deeper masculine envy or fear, to the fulfillment of that ancient desire to create independently of the female, as in the Jewish Golem, the Christian "only-begotten" son, or [Mary] Shelley's modern fantasy, *Frankenstein?* Despite the indisputable fact of the child emerging from the woman's body, for millennia male commentators have been quite ingenious at minimizing her role, for example, claiming that man is the active creator and woman only a passive container. Only in the 1870s, in fact, was it recognized that the woman's egg participated equally in fertilization. But *Brave New World* takes us back to Aristotle, for now men (as scientists) can inform or design the fetus from mere feminine materiality. The biological mother is displaced and her awesome ability to create new life is safely curtailed. Male physicians or "pharmacrats" were already beginning to monopolize childbirth in the West by the 1930s, but in Huxley's future society they have entirely appropriated the maternal function, reducing the female role to Lenina mechanically injecting fetuses in test tubes. In fact, motherhood is made taboo. The worst thing that can happen to a woman in this society is for her to become pregnant and carry a child to term, and there is some evidence that Huxley was in sympathy with his dystopians on this point. The artificiality of the alternative procedure is meant to be shocking, but Huxley also found the intimacy of natural motherhood to be repugnant and even dangerous, especially for the child. Elsewhere in *Brave New World*, the traditional nuclear family is pictured as an unhealthy trap in which mothers are suffocating, domineering, and even sadistic. Perhaps the fact that women lose some of this control through ectogenesis is not so regrettable in Huxley's view, though again female disempowerment is not his explicit focus.

Ectogenesis is possible because women who are fertile sell their ovaries to the State, a transaction that is not very different from prostitutes in our society who also sell parts of their bodies and is something that perhaps anticipates the commercial "stables" of surrogate mothers that have gone into business in recent years. When the women in *Brave New World* feel a void because they can never bear children themselves, they go to the male Dr. Wells (a glance back at H.G. Wells perhaps?) who cheerfully prescribes a chemical "Pregnancy Substitute". But it is not clear that this hormonal treatment is, in fact, an adequate compensation. Without known offspring, these citizens obviously have no close relatives, and sex is generally separated not only from reproduction but also from love. Despite the hectic socializing, each citizen is totally alone. Of course, one might argue that only release from motherhood allows a woman to achieve true equality and avoid the biological essentialism that ties the female identity to her reproductive capacities. But this does not appear to be the case here. Separating sex and reproduction has not freed or empowered these women. Huxley rightly anticipated the profound social impact of the oral birth control pill, and he also assumed, again correctly, as it turned out, that women would bear the burden of contraception. In *Brave New World* 70 percent of females are sterilized and the remaining 30 percent are drilled on how to use the pill; yet men's natural processes are not modified in any way, an imbalance which is not remarked upon in the text. Neither the lot of men nor of women is meant to appear particularly attractive in this, as in any other, dystopia; but what this study has shown is that women are generally worse off than men and only in some instances is this a deliberate portrayal of something which earns Huxley's disapprobation. . . .

In Huxley's works, women have as much opportunity relative to men—at least in theory—in the dystopia *Brave New World* as in the eutopia *Island*; one social arrangement may in its entirety be obviously preferable to the other, but a woman's relative position does not greatly alter. In other words, it is clear that the fate of women alone does not define these societies as eutopian or dystopian, and it is not something to which Huxley pays a great deal of attention. Only on a few occasions does he suggest that women in *Brave New World* are treated differently or more unfairly than the male citizen. In the area of female rights, one might say that Huxley sins more by omission than intention. Perhaps this makes it the more damning; for all his ability to think differently on the technological front, in the underlying sexual politics the more things change, the more they stay the same.

In *Brave New World* Freedom Is Traded for Happiness

George Woodcock

George Woodcock was a Canadian travel writer, poet, essayist, historian, professor, and biographer. He is best known for his travel books and for his controversial book about his friend George Orwell, The Crystal Spirit: A Study of George Orwell.

In the following selection Woodcock suggests that Brave New World *is an expansion of the themes Aldous Huxley covered in* Music at Night, *a volume of essays published in 1931. He asserts that both the novel and the essays are concerned with consumerism, genetic engineering, a youth culture, the danger of too much leisure time, and the rise of a technocracy.*

If any vision runs more persistently than others through Huxley's works, from *Crome Yellow* in 1921 down to *Island* in 1962, it is that of Utopia, the world where a kind of perfection has been attained, change has come to a stop in a temporal parody of eternity. As a young man he saw Utopia as Hell on earth; as an old man he saw it as the earthly paradise. The difference between the two sides of the vision derives from a change in Huxley's views of human potentialities. For the greater part of his life he believed that only a tiny minority was capable of the highest thought or—in later years—of spiritual enlightenment, yet, apart from the brief period when he wrote *Proper Studies*, he distrusted the idea of a world which the elite planned for mankind as a whole. In his final years he believed that he had discovered the way, through mystical discipline and the intelligent use of drugs, to give every man an equal chance of an enlightened existence, and so a Utopia based on a balance of the physical and spiritual, the temporal and eternal, seemed possible to him; such was the vision he gave concrete form in *Island.* . . .

A Didactic Novel

The concept of Utopia, implicitly rejected in *Crome Yellow*, haunted Huxley as he watched the advance of the applied sciences and particularly of physiology and psychology. Utopia, he realized, was not entirely an impossible abstraction. Perhaps it cannot be made with men as they are. But science can change—if not men themselves—at least their attitudes and reactions, and then Utopia becomes feasible as a society in which men cease to be individuals and become merely the components of a social collectivity.

Utopia, of course, is a matter of imposing a pattern, of subordinating human life to a discipline of abstraction analogous to geometry. 'A mind impregnated with music', said Huxley in *Beyond the Mexique Bay*, 'will always tend to impose a pattern on the temporal flux.' But it seemed evident to him that any human attempt to impose an ideal order on Nature or on men would be perverted by man's limitations. So, for all his love of order in geometry and architecture and music, he distrusted it in political or social planning.

Brave New World marks a fundamental change in Huxley's use of the novel; it is no longer fiction intended to describe and satirize. The satirical element remains, but the primary function is now to exhort. Like Orwell's *1984*, *Brave New World* was deliberately devised as a cautionary tale. The earlier novels may have been didactic in part, as *Point Counter Point* clearly was whenever Rampion held the field; *Brave New World* is the first that will be didactic in total intent. This function of the novel, quite apart from any entertainment value it may have as a piece of futurist fantasy, is clearly stated in the description which Huxley gave his father in August 1931: he saw it as

> a comic, or at least satirical, novel about the future, showing the appallingness (at any rate by our standards) of Utopia and adumbrating the effects on thought and feeling of such quite possible biological inventions as the production of children in bottles (with consequent abolition of the family and all the Freudian 'complexes' for which family relationships are responsible), the prolongation of youth, the devising of some harmless but effective substitute for alcohol, cocaine, opium etc:—and also the effects of such sociological reforms on Pavlovian conditions of all children from birth and before birth, universal peace, security and stability.

Peace, Freedom, and the Environment

The shift to openly didactic novel had been presaged by the shift in direction of Huxley's essays. The experience of India and the influence of [author and Huxley's friend D.H.] Lawrence had between them awakened a dormant sense of social responsibility, and from now to the end of his life Huxley was to remain concerned with the fundamental social issues of peace and freedom and the preservation of the environment; even after his conversion to mystical religion he did not retreat out of social responsibility, as many self-styled mystics have done, but remained—even if he did not long continue a political activist—intensely concerned with the plight of man in his temporal existence.

Music at Night, the volume of essays which in 1931 followed the vitalist manifesto of *Do What You Will*, can be read with particular profit as a kind of notebook for *Brave New World*. It discusses a whole series of possibilities which Huxley sees as latent in the European-American world of the late 1920s, and which will form part of the fabric of *Brave New World*: the cult of perpetual youth, the problem of leisure, the

perils of Fordism to the human psyche, the possible development of eugenics as a means of shaping the man of the future, the implications of the attempt to make man primarily a
consumer, and the perils to freedom of a dogmatic egalitari-
anism. A reading of the relevant essays shows that, though
Brave New World is projected on to the screen of the future, it
is derived almost entirely from tendencies which Huxley observed with alarm and distrust in the world around him.

Music at Night is less definite in its expression than *Brave
New World*, for Huxley often presents his possibilities neu-
trally, with the suggestion that men in the future may use
them either for good or for ill. This is the case in his discussion of the ideal drug, which in his essay, 'Wanted, a New
Pleasure', he presents as a possible benefit to mankind. He
suggests endowing a band of research workers to find 'the
ideal intoxicant.'

> If we could sniff or swallow something that would, for five
> or six hours each day, abolish our solitude as individuals,
> atone us with our fellows in a glowing exaltation of affec-
> tion and make life in all its aspects seem not only worth liv-
> ing, but divinely beautiful and significant, and if this heav-
> enly, world-transfiguring drug were of such a kind that we
> could wake up next morning with a clear head and an un-
> damaged constitution—then, it seems to me, all our prob-
> lems (and not merely the one small problem of discovering
> a novel pleasure) would be wholly solved and earth become
> paradise.

This ideal drug will be used both negatively and positively
in Huxley's novels; in *Brave New World* it provides a conditioning technique and its effect is therefore negative and life-
constricting, but in *Island* (written in 1962 after Huxley had
experimented with LSD) it is used in a positive Utopia as part
of a technique of mental liberation. . . .

Perils of Passionless Happiness

As we have seen, *Brave New World* projects happiness as the principal goal of Utopia and equals it with non-freedom. The society of the future is a parody of Plato's republic, with a small group of World Controllers ruling five castes of subjects, divided not merely socially but biologically, since they have been conditioned to their future tasks in the bottles where they were bred. To preserve happiness, the World Controllers throw away everything that might provoke either thought or passion.

> The world's stable now [says Mustapha Mond, Controller for England]. People are happy; they get what they want, and they never want what they can't get. They're well off; they're safe; they're never ill; they're not afraid of death; they're blissfully ignorant of passion and old age; they're plagued with no mothers or fathers; they've got no wives, or children, or lovers to feel strongly about; they're so conditioned that they practically can't help behaving as they ought to behave.

The most striking difference between *Brave New World* and *1984*, with which it has so often been compared, is the absence of violence and overt repression.

> In the end [says Mond] the Controllers realized that force was no good. The slower but infinitely surer methods of ectogenesis, neo-Pavlovian conditions, and hypnopaedia. . . .

Men are so conditioned from the time the spermatozoon enters the egg in the Hatchery that there is little likelihood of their breaking into rebellion; if they do become discontented there are always drugs to waft them into the heavens of restorative illusion. Thus the Controllers are able to govern with a softly firm hand; the police use whiffs of anaesthetic instead of truncheons, and those over-brilliant individuals who do not fit the established pattern are allowed to indulge their heretical notions in the intellectual quarantine of exile.

The daily lives of the conditioned inhabitants of the brave new world are passed in a carefully regulated pattern of production and consumption. Since it was found that too much leisure created restlessness, scientists are discouraged from devising labour-saving inventions, and the working day is followed by gregarious pleasures so organized that elaborate machinery is required and maximum consumption is encouraged. Complete freedom of sexual behaviour, plus the availability of soma, provide releases from all ordinary frustrations. The abolition of viviparous birth has made families and all other permanent attachments unnecessary; individuals have become merely cells, each occupying his special position in the carefully differentiated fabric of society.

All this would not make a novel of its own; Utopian fiction that merely describes a futuristic society is notoriously tedious. Huxley brings his to life by showing the perils of any attempt at a perfect society. The higher castes of the community, the Alphas and the Betas, cannot be as closely conditioned as the worker castes, because their tasks involve intelligence and the occasional need to use judgement; and even the best conditioning is not foolproof. So we get sports like the stunted Bernard Marx who has a heretical longing for solitude, like the pneumatic Lenina Crowne who is inclined to remain a little too constant in her attachments, like Helmholtz Watson who secretly writes forbidden poems about the self instead of slogans for the state.

Science vs. Primitivism

Bernard is already suspected of disaffection and threatened with exile to Iceland, but the crisis in the life of all these three misfits in Utopia is provoked—like crises in Huxley's own life—by a journey into unfamiliarity. Bernard takes Lenina on a trip to the reservation for primitive people in New Mexico. For Lenina the first sight of dirt and disease is traumatic, but Bernard is rewarded by the discovery of a woman from Utopia who was lost years ago and has since lived and brought up her child among the Indians. The young man—John—is not only a savage; he has also, accidentally, acquired a copy of Shakespeare which, with the mixed heathen and Christian cults of the Indians, has enriched his language and shaped his outlook. In our sense he is far more 'cultured', if not more 'civilized', than the utopians.

Bernard brings the savage back to London, where he creates a sensation by his baroque behaviour and Elizabethan speech. On Bernard and Helmholtz he has the effect of crystallizing their sense of difference from the society to which they have been bred. Lenina, who is merely a Beta Plus and therefore not so inclined to intellectual rebellion, lapses into an old-fashioned infatuation for the savage, who meanwhile has conceived a romantic attachment to her. There is an extraordinarily comic scene of crossed purposes, in which the savage declares his love in resounding Shakespearian terms, whereupon Lenina, reacting in the only way she knows, unzips her garments and advances upon him in all her pneumatic nakedness, and the savage, shouting Elizabethan curses, drives her from him.

The rebellion, slight as it is, fails. The three young men, Bernard, Helmholtz and the savage, after creating a minor riot by interrupting a distribution of soma, are brought before Mustapha Mond. There is a Peacockian [after author Thomas Love Peacock] interlude in which each of the four characteristically reacts to the situation, and then Bernard and Helmholtz are exiled to join those who have shown themselves unreliable in the past (the real intellectual elite of the brave new world). The savage is forbidden to join them, because Mond wants to continue the experiment of subjecting him to 'civilization'. Since he cannot go anywhere else, the savage tries to establish a hermitage in the Surrey countryside of Huxley's youth, but Utopia's equivalents of newshounds discover him, and the fervent pleasure-seekers of the brave new world, hearing that he is flogging himself like a New Mexican penitent, descend on him in their helicopters. Lenina is among them. There is a great orgy in which the savage first whips and then possesses her. The next day, revolted by Utopia and his surrender to its seductions, he hangs himself.

In thematic terms, *Brave New World* opposes the scientific-industrialist ideal of Mustapha Mond (and, by derivation, of Henry Ford) to the primitivist vitalism of Lawrence, the acceptance of life with all its joys and miseries, as it exists. A decade later Huxley criticized himself for having failed to add a third possibility, that of the decentralized, libertarian society, where industry is minimized and man is liberated to pursue the life of time by the illumination of eternity. Yet it is difficult to see how the novel could have been changed to include this third possibility. The anti-individualist tendencies latent in our society have to be opposed by the poetic primitivism of the savage, who alone, since he is the only character conscious of the nature of tragedy, can embody the tragic possibilities of man's future.

One is tempted to consider *Brave New World*, because it is a Utopian fantasy, as an exceptional work that stands outside the general pattern of Aldous Huxley's fiction. In reality, its function is to close the sequence of the earlier novels. The central characters belong clearly in the Huxleian succession. Bernard is a latter-day Gumbril who has to inflate himself perpetually in order to feel equal to others, and who can only fulfil himself in exceptional circumstances. Helmholtz is a Calamy, an expert amorist who has lost his taste for sensual delights and longs for something more elevated and intelligent. The savage is a more acceptable vehicle for the Lawrencian viewpoint than the excessively didactic Rampion. And Mustapha Mond, with his orotund delivery, is a Scogan or a Cardan who has at last made good. As for the world of the novel, it is the Bohemia of *Antic Hay* and *Point Counter Point*, carried to its logical end, its pleasures sanctified and its personal irresponsibilities institutionalized so that the freedom of the libertine is revealed as the most insidious of slaveries. There can be no doubt of the continuity between *Brave New World* and the earlier novels. It is the direction of the journey that has changed.

Huxley Presents a Choice Between Imperfect Humanity and Perfect Biotechnology

Leon R. Kass

Leon R. Kass is an American physician, scientist, professor, and author. He is the Addie Clark Harding Professor in the Committee on Social Thought and the College at the University of Chicago and the Hertog Fellow at the American Enterprise Institute. Kass served as chairman of the President's Council on Bioethics from 2001 to 2005, during the presidency of George W. Bush. His tenure was controversial because of his opposition to cloning and his criticism of embryonic stem cell research.

In the following viewpoint Kass compares the human enhancement technologies available in 2000 with Aldous Huxley's vision in Brave New World. *He finds Huxley remarkably prescient in predicting the scientific advances that can perfect life and offer happiness, and also in suggesting that the price will be a diminishment of humanity and liberty.*

The urgency of the great political struggles of the twentieth century, successfully waged against totalitarianisms first right [fascism] and then left [communism], seems to have blinded many people to a deeper truth about the present age: all contemporary societies, the open ones no less than the closed, are traveling briskly in the same utopian direction. All are wedded to the modern technological project; all march eagerly to the drums of progress and fly proudly the banner of modern science; all sing loudly the Baconian [after English Elizabethan scientist and philosopher Francis Bacon] anthem, "Conquer nature, relieve man's estate."

Leon R. Kass, "Aldous Huxley: *Brave New World* (1932)," *First Things: A Monthly Journal of Religion and Public Life*, March 2000, p. 51. Copyright © 2000 Institute on Religion and Public Life. All rights reserved. Reproduced by permission.

Power to Enhance Human Nature

Leading the triumphal procession is modern medicine, the epitome of compassionate humanitarianism, becoming every day ever more powerful in its battle against disease, decay, and death, thanks especially to the astonishing achievements in biomedical science and technology—achievements for which we must surely be grateful. Yet contemplating present and projected advances in genetic and reproductive technologies, in neuroscience and psychopharmacology, and in the development of artificial organs and computer-chip implants for human brains, we now clearly recognize new uses for biotechnical power that soar beyond the traditional medical goals of healing disease and relieving suffering. Human nature itself lies on the operating table, ready for alteration, "enhancement," and wholesale redesign.

Some transforming powers are already here. The pill. In vitro fertilization. Bottled embryos. Surrogate wombs. Cloning. Genetic screening. Organ harvests. Mechanical spare parts. Chimeras. Brain implants. Ritalin for the young, Viagra for the old, and Prozac for everyone. And, to leave this vale of tears, a little extra morphine accompanied by Muzak. What? You still have troubles? Not to worry. As the vaudevillians used to say, "You ain't seen nothin' yet!"

The Price of Genetic Engineering

Years ago Aldous Huxley saw it coming. More important, he knew what it meant and, in his charming but disturbing novel, *Brave New World*, Huxley made it strikingly visible for all to see. *Brave New World* is not a great book, and, in purely literary terms, even the author found it seriously flawed. Yet, in my experience, its power increases with each rereading, and coming generations of readers should—and I hope will—find it still more compelling. For unlike other frightening futuristic novels of the past century, such as Orwell's already dated *Nineteen Eighty-four*, Huxley shows us a dystopia that goes with, rather than against, the human grain—indeed, it is animated by modernity's most humane and progressive aspirations. Following those aspirations to their ultimate realization, Huxley enables us to recognize those less obvious but often more pernicious evils that are inextricably linked to successful attainment of partial goods. And he strongly suggests that we must choose: either our misery-ridden but still richly human world, or the squalid happiness of the biotechnical world to come.

In this satirical novel, Huxley paints human life seven centuries hence, living under the gentle hand of a compassionate humanitarianism that has been rendered fully competent by genetic manipulation, psychopharmacology, hypnopaedia, and high-tech amusements. At long last, mankind has succeeded in eliminating disease, aggression, war, pain, anxiety, suffering, hatred, guilt, envy, and grief. But this victory comes at a heavy price: homogenization, mediocrity, pacification, spurious contentment, trivial pursuits, shallow attachments, debasement of tastes, and souls without loves or longings.

The Brave New World has achieved prosperity, community, stability, and nigh-universal contentment, only to be peopled by creatures of human shape but of stunted humanity. They consume, fornicate, take "soma" and "violent passion surrogate," enjoy "Riemann-surface tennis" and "centrifugal bumble-puppy," and operate the machinery that makes it all possible. They do not read, write, think, love, or govern themselves. Creativity and curiosity, reason and passion, exist only in a rudimentary and mutilated form. Art and science, virtue and religion, family and friendship are all passé. What matters most is present satisfaction: "Never put off till tomorrow the fun you can have today." Like Midas, brave new man will be cursed to acquire precisely what he wished for only to discover—painfully and too late—that what he wished for is not exactly what he wanted. Or, Huxley implies, worse than Midas, he may be so dehumanized that he will not even recognize that in aspiring to be perfect he is no longer even human.

Huxley's Predictions Coming True

Huxley's novel is, of course, science fiction. But yesterday's science fiction is rapidly becoming today's fact. Prozac is not yet Huxley's soma; cloning by nuclear transfer or splitting embryos is not exactly Bokanovskification; MTV and virtual-reality parlors are not quite the "feelies"; and our current safe-and-consequenceless sexual practices are not universally as loveless or as empty as in the novel. But the kinships are disquieting, all the more so since our technologies of bio-psycho-engineering are still in their infancy—and it is all too clear what they might look like in their full maturity. Indeed, the cultural changes technology has already wrought among us should make us even more worried than Huxley would have us be.

In Huxley's novel, everyone without exception is genetically programmed and psychologically conditioned, beginning even before birth, under the direction of an omnipotent—albeit benevolent—world state. Accordingly, for Huxley, it is lack of freedom that will be the major price of engineered "perfection," including the freedom to be unhappy. But the dehumanization he portrays does not really require despotism or external control. To the contrary, precisely because the society of the future will deliver exactly what people most want—health, safety, comfort, plenty, pleasure, peace of mind, and length of days—mankind can reach the same humanly debased condition solely on the basis of free human choice. No need for World Controllers. Just give us the technological imperative, liberal democratic society, compassionate humanitarianism, moral pluralism, and free markets, and we can take ourselves to Brave New World all by ourselves. If you require evidence, just look around.

In our age of cultural unraveling and dissolving moral agreement, it is heartening that readers are still revolted by Huxley's picture of the life to which, absent some moral and religious reawakening, our cherished prejudices will take us. While philosophical essays and moral exhortation are today largely impotent, good literature can—at least for now—capture our impoverished imaginations and thus keep the human flame aflicker.

The Brave New World Already Exists

Rebecca West

Rebecca West was a celebrated British novelist, journalist, literary critic, biographer, social satirist, and travel writer. When she was in her twenties she had a relationship with author H.G. Wells that resulted in the birth of their son, Anthony West. She is the author of the novels The Return of the Soldier *and* The Birds Fall Down.

In the following selection, from a book review of Brave New World *published in 1932, West states that* Brave New World *is based on the chapter "The Grand Inquisitor" in Fyodor Dostoevsky's* The Brothers Karamazov. *Just as Dostoevsky was denouncing the religious intolerance of the Inquisition, Aldous Huxley is attacking a society that ceases to ponder the great questions about existence. West considers* Brave New World *to be an important novel. Her only criticism is that Huxley fails to make clear that his Brave New World actually exists: scientific and social experiments like the ones he describes were being conducted when he wrote the book.*

Those who are easily shocked had better leave Mr. Aldous Huxley's new fantasy, *Brave New World*, on one side; noting, as they pass, that since this is a free country they are not compelled to read it.

Those who are not easily shocked can settle down to enjoy what is not only the most accomplished novel Mr. Huxley has yet written, but also the most serious religious work written for some years. His tendency in his other novels has been to select subject matter which might fairly be described as a fuss about nothing. Even the characters in *Point Counter Point* were carefully docketed as interesting individuals—they were, in relation to the depicted imbroglio, as lacking in allure as sexually-maladjusted cockroaches. But the argument in *Brave New World* is of major importance. One could sanely ask for nothing more than it gives.

Based on Reality

One would say that the book was about a Utopia if it were not that a line of dreamers have given that originally noncommittal term a sense of imagined perfection; for the book describes the world as Mr. Huxley sees it may become if certain modern tendencies grow dominant and its character is rather of a deduced abomination.

If one has a complaint to make against him it is that he does not explain to the reader in a preface or footnotes how much solid justification he has for his horrid visions. It would add to the reader's interest if he knew that when Mr. Huxley depicts the human race as abandoning its viviparous habits and propagating by means of germ cells surgically removed from the body and fertilised in laboratories (so that the embryo develops in a bottle and is decanted instead of born) he is writing of a possibility that biologists are seeing not more remotely than, let us say, Leonardo da Vinci saw the aeroplane. And it would add to the reader's sympathetic horror if he realised that the society which Mr. Huxley represents as being founded on this basis is actually the kind of society that various living people, notably in America and Russia, and in connection with the Bolshevist and Behaviourist movements, have expressed a desire to establish; and that this is true even of the least pleasing details.

There is, for instance, one incident which immensely enhances the impressiveness of the book if one knows its counter-part in reality.

In this new world there are various grades of human beings to do various work, ranging from Alphas, who hold all the positions of power and do all the intellectual work, to the Epsilons, who do all the drudgery and are too stupid to read or write. These are all bred for the purpose from selected germ-cells, exposed to various treatments during their bottled stages, and then educated by various devices depending on the theory of the 'conditioned reflex', which holds that any animal or human being can be taught to dislike an object, even if inherently pleasing, if it is always presented to them in association with an object that is inherently unpleasing to them. Mr. Huxley gives an example of one of these devices. . . .

This device serves two purposes. Since the Deltas have to perform fairly intricate work they cannot be bred below a certain fairly high level of intelligence, above that which would make it possible for them to read or write; but since the community cannot afford to have them waste their time on what must necessarily be a fourth-rate mental life, it seeks to make books hateful to them. And it has to discourage any native love of flowers, because they are not machine-made; and the appetite of citizens must be directed away from the natural to machine-made goods, so that the nightmare of overproduction may be laid for ever.

Now the interesting thing about this experiment is that it is in technique exactly the same as those constantly conducted by Dr. John B. Watson, the founder of Behaviourism, a philosophy which has probably made more adherents in the last twenty years than Christian Science did in the last twenty years of the nineteenth century, and finds them in a more influential grade.

I hope some time to try out the experiment of having a
table top electrically wired in such a way that if a child
reaches for a glass or a delicate vase, it will be punished,

whereas if it reaches for its toys or other things it is allowed to play with, it can get them without being electrically shocked.

He believes in 'building in the negative reactions demanded by society'; and the society he belongs to is one that would certainly, if it could, have demanded such reactions as Mr. Huxley's new world demanded from the Deltas. Was it not that society in which, just before the Wall Street crash [of 1929], a conference of automobile manufacturers expressed an intention of 'stimulating the two-car sense'?

There is, indeed, nothing at all impossible in Mr. Huxley's vision of a world where the infants are conditioned by such experiments, and by the dormitory loud speakers that whisper moral education into their sleeping ears (his pages on hypno-paædia, or sleep-teaching, are among the most amusing in the book) into a lack of all characteristics save those which tend to uphold the stability of the State. Much of it is actual in America.

A World of Emptiness

There is this salesmanship, which enjoins them to make a division between that which is valued and that which is preserved; they are taught to acquire an infinity of gimcrack objects, display them, throw them away. They are taught to dissipate their force on silly crowd pleasures. The talkies have become the feelies—they feel the kisses and the tears—but have not changed their fatuous essence. The chemists have found that drug they have been looking for, which intoxicates without deleterious effect on the nervous system. Leisure hours, therefore, become a blandly drunken petting-party; for promiscuity is a social duty, since it discourages far more than puritanism the growth of that disintegrating factor, love.

The religious instinct has been transferred by skilful conditioning to a deity known as Our Ford, whose beautiful and inspired sayings such as 'History is bunk' are reverently handed down. Age has disappeared, youth is artificially prolonged till 60, when there comes death, which is not feared. We are privileged to visit now a co-educational establishment under the headship of Miss Keate, a freemartin [sterile woman], and see five 'busloads of her pupils singing or in silent embracement', rolling home from Slough Crematorium for a stage in the death conditioning which begins at eighteen months.

Every tot spends two mornings a week in a hospital for the dying. All the best toys are kept there, and they get chocolate creams on death days. They learn to take dying as a matter of course. Emotional and intellectual life is entirely flattened out, so that the State which supplies the material needs of the citizens shall run with a triumphant smoothness, as it is intended in Bolshevist Russia. If the individual is drowned, at least he is drowned in a bath of communal happiness.

Into this world comes a Savage: a white child who has been born, through certain odd circumstances, in an American Indian reservation which has been kept untouched for psychological research reasons. His mind is governed by the harsh conceptions of Indian religion. He believes in the vileness of man that can be made acceptable to the gods only by fasting and scourging, and again scourging; so that blood must be drawn from the back if the gods are to let rain fall on the pueblo and the corn grow; and the delights of love must be fenced away by restriction upon restriction, and cancelled afterwards by shuddering loathing of them and contempt for the object who afforded them.

Towards those who begot or conceived one (so obscenely, compared with the decent technique of bottling and decanting) one is fixed in a torturing relationship of loving concern which it is almost impossible to destroy.

Far from blood and hatred and anguished passion being eliminated from life, they are ritually preserved; and nothing is done to veil the threat that, at the end of all this agony, there is nothing but a door painfully opening into emptiness.

To this harsh existence there are no palliatives save the joy to be found in hunting and dancing, in the craftsmanship of the potter and the weaver: unserviceable æsthetic joys. It happens that the Savage has found in the Indian reservation an old volume containing the works of Shakespeare, an author forbidden in the new world on account of the reprehensibly private nature of the emotions he chiefly describes. They supply him with an almost complete language to express these blood-stained primitive beliefs; since the poet, also, for all that the literature teachers have done to disguise it (as one may read in an entertaining essay by Mr. Lytton Strachey), held beliefs not very different.

The Savage is, therefore, aware of his own world. It is not merely strangeness that makes him detest the new world and use the more denunciatory passages from Shakespeare to express what he thinks about its arrangement.

He finds contentment everywhere, but no nobility. Relief from the fear of death is no gain. As he sees his mother die in the Hospital for the Dying ('something between a first-class hotel and a feely palace, if you take my meaning,' says the nurse) doped with the new drug, canned music, and perfumes, while Epsilon dwarf twins munch chocolate eclairs round her bed as part of their death-conditioning treatment, he realises that to know the terror of death is better than to be drugged out of that knowledge. As he says when he talks to Mustapha Mond, one of the ten World Controllers (a cynic who reads Shakespeare, too, behind locked doors), things are too easy. One pays no price and one gets nothing valuable. He quotes Othello, 'If after every tempest come such calms, may the winds blow till they have wakened death.'

A Rewrite of *The Brothers Karamazov*

It is only at the end of the book that one sees precisely what literary task Mr. Aldous Huxley has set himself. He has rewritten in terms of our age the chapter called 'The Grand

Inquisitor' in *The Brothers Karamazov*. In these days Dostoevsky is out of fashion, partly because he writes with heat and passion of the sort that Mr. T.S. Eliot's sham classicism has taught us to despise, and partly because the simple and elephant-sized neuroses of [Russian author Leo] Tolstoy are easier for the inattentive eye to follow than the subtle spiritual ferments of Dostoevsky. But 'The Grand Inquisitor' is a symbolic statement that every generation ought to read afresh. In it Christ revisits earth, works a miracle in the streets of Seville, and is immediately, by order of the Cardinal, thrown into the prisons of the Inquisition.

The Cardinal visits the captive in the middle of the night and tells him that he has recognised him as the Christ, but means to burn him at the stake, because he insists on the freedom of man, and man cannot be happy unless he is a slave. 'For now' (he is speaking of the Inquisition, of course) 'for the first time it has become possible to think of the happiness of men. Man was created a rebel; and how can rebels be happy?'

The words are almost the same as Mr. Huxley's World Controller's. But instead of the Inquisition, instead of the orthodoxy that in the nineteenth century crushed spiritual endeavour, Mr. Huxley is attacking the new spirit which tries to induce man to divert in continual insignificant movements relating to the material framework of life all his force, and to abandon the practice of speculating about his existence and his destiny. Equally a denunciation of Capitalism and Communism so far as they discourage man from thinking freely, it is a declaration that art is a progressive revelation of the universe to man, and that those who interfere with it leave men to die miserably in the night of ignorance.

The book is many other things as well. One could cover many columns with discussion of its implications. It is, indeed, almost certainly one of the half-dozen most important books that have been published since the war.

Huxley's Predictions on Technology Were Remarkably Accurate

The Economist

Published weekly since 1843, The Economist *provides analysis of global business news and current events.*

Aldous Huxley made predictions about the organization of society and the technologies that would be employed in the future in Brave New World. *In the following selection from* The Economist, *the author finds it interesting that Huxley got more of the technological predictions right, because these would have been more difficult to predict. Among the technologies Huxley foretold were virtual reality, in vitro fertilization, and cloning.*

Things are not nearly as bleak as Aldous Huxley predicted in 1932 in *Brave New World*. Parenthood has not been generally abolished; the best toys are not kept at the crematorium; the north pole is not home to a bad hotel called the Aurora Bora Palace. Yet his satirical depiction of human enslavement to the twin masters of medical technology and capitalism is still prescient enough to sting—not least because he foresaw the power of modern biology 20 years before the discovery of the structure of DNA.

The novel opens at the Central London Hatchery, where a batch of eager students of higher than average intelligence are being shown around by the Director of Hatcheries and Conditioning. The tour begins at the Fertilising Room where eggs and sperm have been collected and are being mixed together.

The Economist, "Scientific Brutality: Aldous Huxley's Bleak Vision," *The Economist,* vol. 346, no. 8057, February 28, 1998, p. 86. Copyright © 1998 by Economist Newspaper Ltd. Republished with permission of *The Economist,* conveyed through Copyright Clearance Center, Inc.

Then the students watch while, in the Social Predestination Room, embryos designated to grow into intelligent adults—the alphas and betas—are left to develop in peace ("one egg, one embryo, one adult").

Those embryos destined by their genes to be menial labourers are split, and then split again, as many times as possible—cloned, in other words, albeit using what Huxley dubs "Bokanovsky's Process", or what scientists call embryo-splitting—to give rise to huge batches of identical twins. These poor embryos—the gammas, deltas and epsilons—are deliberately subjected to increasingly poor environments to ensure stupidity and stunting, and to minimise variation between individuals.

Ghastly stuff. But worse is to come. The eager students go on to see the nurseries, where children are fed with an artificial "external secretion", conditioned with electric shocks to turn away from knowledge, and brain-washed as they sleep with the endless whisperings of the ultimate consumer society ("ending is better than mending, ending is better than mending, I love new clothes, I love new clothes").

As the plot unfolds, the novel makes predictions of two kinds: first, about the way that society will be organised and, second, about technologies that will be widely used. The second predictions are the more interesting—not only because Huxley got more of them right, but also because from his vantage point, 65 years ago, they would have been far more surprising.

The first transatlantic flights were not attempted until the 1920s. The first fully electronic television set was not unveiled until 1932. The contraceptive pill was not invented until the 1950s. Yet Huxley imagined a world in which flights between London and Santa Fe take 6 hours and where televisions are not only in every room but even at the end of the beds of people dying in nursing homes. Girls at school are subject to "Malthusian drill" in contraceptive use; and there is abortion on demand (indeed by decree) if the contraceptives fail. In addition, everybody is immunised (while still in the bottle) against infectious diseases.

In *Brave New World*, Huxley also foresaw virtual reality. True, nobody goes to the "feelies" instead of the movies, but it is probably just a matter of time before "feelies" arrive. More impressively, he foresaw the new technologies of reproductive biology, such as the ability to achieve fertilisation outside the womb. He imagined a way to clone people (embryo-splitting) that is different from the one that brought Dolly the Sheep into the world. Embryo-splitting can already be done, and has been used to create human twins, or clones, born years apart. Their parents (donors?) presumably hope that they will grow to be alphas or betas.

Huxley's Predictions of Loss of Liberty Were Not Accurate

John Derbyshire

John Derbyshire is a British-born writer currently living in the United States. He writes for the National Review *and* New English Review *on a variety of social and political topics.*

In the following viewpoint Derbyshire disputes the relevance of Brave New World *to today's world. In actual practice, biotechnology has been used to improve the lot of humanity, not to curtail civil liberties, he contends. Both Aldous Huxley and George Orwell were reacting to the concerns of their era, but those concerns are not valid today. The threats to individual freedoms that they warned against have not come to pass, Derbyshire asserts, and their books are period pieces.*

This year [2007] marks the 75th birthday of Aldous Huxley's novel *Brave New World*, first published in February 1932. That novel became one of the most discussed works of literature of the 20th century. Its title, which Huxley took from Shakespeare's play *The Tempest*, has passed into the language—from Huxley, not from Shakespeare—as a descriptor for any development, or any imagined future, based on biotechnological attempts to enhance or transform human nature, or even just nature. In vitro fertilization? Brave new world! Stem-cell research? Brave new world! Genetically modified crops? Brave new world! The title of Huxley's novel has become a scare phrase brandished at any intervention by science in the fundamental processes of life. Is this fair to the book? Does the book have anything useful to tell us, or any warning to give us, as we peer into our own future?

John Derbyshire, "Huxley's Period Piece: *Brave New World* Turns 75," *National Review,* vol. 59, no. 3, March 5, 2007, pp. 38–41. Copyright © 2007 by National Review, Inc., 215 Lexington Avenue, New York, NY 10016. Reproduced by permission.

Two Great Visions

Brave New World was one of two great visions of the future as imagined by two Englishmen who came to maturity in the early years of the 20th century. Huxley, born in 1894, was the older of the two. George Orwell, younger by nine years, was of course the author of *Nineteen Eight-Four*, which described a future quite different from Huxley's, and much nearer to the author's own time.

In the later 20th century it was common for high-school seniors to be told to read both Huxley's book and Orwell's, then to write an essay comparing the two visions and passing an opinion on which future was more probable. I recall doing this myself. Some dichotomies came easily to mind. Orwell was thinking about the 1940s USSR [the Soviet Union]; Huxley, about the 1920s USA. (The novel was perceived by many as anti-American, and was reviewed less favorably here than in England.) In Orwell's dystopia the human spirit had been raped; in Huxley's, it had been seduced. . . . And so on.

The general opinion was that Huxley's imagined future was more probable than Orwell's. This was especially the case after the fall of the USSR and the end of the Maoist despotism in China had cast doubt on the idea that a terroristic totalitarianism of the *Nineteen Eighty-Four* type could sustain itself indefinitely (a doubt perhaps not shared by the citizens of Cuba or North Korea). The new understanding of genetics brought by [James] Watson and [Francis] Crick's analysis of DNA, followed by the work of [Robert] Trivers, [William] Hamilton, and [Margo] Wilson on the evolutionary underpinnings of behavior, also turned people's thoughts toward a future in which human nature was manipulated, rather than brutalized, into submission.

A Similar Worldview

Now, from our longer perspective, the similarities of the books are more striking than their differences. Both show human beings bereft of liberty. Both show a coarse popular culture triumphant—the propaganda movies, machine-written novels, and vapid pop songs of *Nineteen Eighty-Four*, the "feelies" and electromagnetic golf of *Brave New World*. Most telling, both portray static, "end of history" worlds, in which all change has ceased, along with the quest for knowledge.

In a letter dated September 15, 1931, when he must have been finishing up *Brave New World*, Huxley wrote:

> I have been very much preoccupied with a difficult piece of work—a Swiftian novel about the Future, showing the horrors of Utopia and the strange and appalling effects on feeling, "instinct" and general weltanschauung [worldview] of the application of psychological, physiological and mechanical knowledge to the fundamentals of human life. It is a comic book—but seriously comic.

The word "Utopia" there would have been taken by any literate person of the time to refer to the later works of H.G. Wells, especially the 1923 novel *Men Like Gods*, in which a party of Englishmen is accidentally transported into a parallel world run on Wellsian principles, a "universal scientific state" actually named Utopia, where all are made happy and well-adjusted via free love, eugenics, and enlightened education.

Wells, born in 1866, was of the generation before Huxley and Orwell, a generation for which unbounded late-Victorian scientific optimism was still possible. The younger writers, speaking from the dissolution and pessimism that followed World War I, understood that there was something wrong with Wells's dream of progress and harmony under benevolent technocratic elites, and were intent on telling us what that something was.

All three of these books—Wells's, Huxley's, and Orwell's—contain a dialectical passage in which the central issues of these imagined worlds are batted back and forth between a skeptical "normal" man of the author's time and a proponent of the new order. In *Men Like Gods*, one of the Englishmen accuses a Utopian of having thrown out the baby with the bathwater: "Life on earth was, he admitted, insecure, full of pains and anxieties, full indeed of miseries and distresses and anguish, but also, and indeed by reason of these very things, it had moments of intensity, hopes, joyful surprises, escapes, attainments, such as the ordered life of Utopia could not possibly afford." This being Wells, the Utopian easily swats down these antique cavils.

In *Nineteen Eighty-Four* the equivalent metaphysical exchange is between Winston Smith and O'Brien in the Ministry of Love: "Does Big Brother exist?" "Of course he exists. The Party exists . . ." Etc.

Huxley's dialectic comes at the end of Chapter 17 in *Brave New World*. Mustapha Mond, the Controller for Western Europe, is in conversation with John the Savage, who knows his Shakespeare:

"Exposing what is mortal and unsure to all that fortune, death and danger dare, even for an egg-shell. Isn't there something in that?" [John] asked, looking up at Mustapha Mond. "Quite apart from God—though of course God would be a reason for it. Isn't there something in living dangerously?"

"There's a great deal in it," the Controller replied. "Men and women must have their adrenals stimulated from time to time."

"What?" questioned the Savage, uncomprehending.

"It's one of the conditions of perfect health. That's why we've made the V.P.S. treatments compulsory."

"V.P.S.?"

"Violent Passion Surrogate. Regularly once a month. We flood the whole system with adrenin. It's the complete physiological equivalent of fear and rage. All the tonic effects of murdering Desdemona and being murdered by Othello, without any of the inconveniences."

"But I like the inconveniences."

"We don't," said the Controller. "We prefer to do things comfortably."

It is at about this point that the reader of *Brave New World* finds himself, at least momentarily, wondering just what, exactly, is wrong with life in the World State. Every citizen is happy, safe, and employed in work suitable to his abilities. Whatever need human beings may have for danger and excitement can be satisfied by a shot of Violent Passion Surrogate. Such minor forms of unhappiness as might arise can be banished with a gram of soma. What's not to like? The philosophical issues here are nontrivial.

A less disturbing question is whether, in fact, this degree of manipulation of human nature is possible. Almost certainly it is not. The notion that by careful breeding and sufficiently intensive conditioning you can get people to behave in any way at all is very mid-20th-century. The modern view of human nature, being gradually uncovered by researches in evolutionary genetics and neuroscience, is more earthily biological. Our brains appear to have been structured by the rigors of natural selection to believe and desire certain things, and not certain other things. The human personality is not infinitely malleable: The Old Adam is hard-wired into it, and no amount of conditioning can reliably expel him. Men cannot be like gods.

This suggests that the power structure of the World State, and of its Wellsian and Orwellian equivalents, is unstable. C.S. Lewis made this point in *The Abolition of Man*: "I am inclined to think that the Conditioners will hate the conditioned." (Lewis was not writing about Huxley's book, though he must have had it in mind.) He was surely right. The urge to power would likely survive even into a world like Huxley's, in which

Ensemble members perform an adaptation of Huxley's Brave New World *in 2006 at the Grips Theatre in Berlin.* AP Images.

there is little need for the Controllers to exercise power. They would become corrupted in any case, as the Inner Party of Orwell's nightmare world would, as human beings always will, so long as they are recognizably human.

Huxley's Biotech Not Relevant

What, then, are the answers to the questions I started out with? Is it fair to Huxley's book to attach its title to our fears about biotechnology? Does *Brave New World* have anything to tell us about our own future?

I would answer both questions in the negative. While it is certainly conceivable that a ruthlessly despotic state might turn biotechnology to malign uses, the general trend of bio-technological advance in our time is to expand the sphere of human liberty. Ronald Bailey has spelled this out in his excellent book *Liberation Biology*. Longer lifespans; the conquest of disease; transplants from limbs and organs grown in vitro; "designer babies"—every one of these developments ought to be welcomed by free citizens in a free society.

Even for those who would dispute Bailey's optimism, the biotechnology of Huxley's world is not very relevant. When the mass-production assembly line was a new thing, the cloning of low-caste embryos might have made some economic sense. In the robotized factories of today, it would not. Even less relevant to present-day concerns is hypnopaedic suggestion, the key method of socialization in *Brave New World*. The problem here is that hypnopaedic suggestion does not, and cannot, work. The sleeping brain is simply not receptive to learning.

The only feature of Huxley's World State that resonates today is the widespread use of soma to relieve psychic discomfort. Any pharmacist will tell you that mild anti-depressants are among his best-moving items. This is still some way from *Brave New World*, though. Soma-strength narcotics can be obtained by any American who wants them badly enough. Few do. The 1960s call to "turn on, tune in, drop out" had little appeal or staying power. Lotus-eating is not actually very popular. Most of us would rather remain engaged with life. (Though Huxley himself answered the 1960s siren call in his last hours. Dying from cancer, he asked for, and was given, LSD, and died under the influence.)

Taking *Brave New World* to be a cautionary tale about the perils of scientific inquiry is even more wrongheaded. While Huxley's dystopia depends on some minor technological advances, its spirit is essentially anti-scientific. The author, who knew his science—he was the grandson of T.H. Huxley, the great Victorian biologist—makes this plain. "Every change is a menace to stability," the Controller tells the Savage in their dialogue. "Every discovery in pure science is potentially subversive." Huxley's imagined world, like Orwell's, is static. We are not being shown the perils of letting science march on indefinitely, so much as the perils of letting science march forward a short distance, then stop forever.

In this respect, the Utopians in H.G. Wells's *Men Like Gods* are, for all their icy Houyhnhnmish complacency [a reference to Houyhnhnms, a race of horses in Jonathan Swift's *Gulliver's Travels*, that represent rational existence], at least dynamic; they are planning the conquest of outer space, for instance. Huxley and Orwell offered fantasies of stasis—really just sour versions of the ancient millenarian dream: the City of the Sun, the Great Harmony, Developed Socialism, Year Zero, the Kingdom of Heaven on Earth.

Not Relevant Today

Brave New World is at last a period piece. Huxley could not know what a disaster the command economy, first field-tested in World War I, would turn out to be. He glimpsed the vision of managerial elites indifferent to ideology—the elites described in detail by James Burnham a decade later, and given fictional flesh in Orwell's 1949 masterpiece. In most of the world, however, those elites found that the assumption of total power, far from advancing their interests, was ultimately fatal to them, and they came to a quiet understanding with constitutional democracy or some rough approximation thereof.

Huxley and Orwell were men of their place and time. They both had memories of the old order in England—the era of casual liberty and minimal government that ended with what people of their generation called the Great War. As the golden glow of that memory faded, and the mid-century shadows lengthened, they looked with fear and despair to an age without liberty.

Their fears were misplaced. Somehow we have held on to our old freedoms. If we keep our wits about us, we may carry them forward intact into the future—a future in which, 75 years from now, our current fears of eco-catastrophe, biotech disasters, and nuclear terrorism may seem as quaint as soma, the Hatcheries, and the College of Emotional Engineering.

Social Issues in Literature

CHAPTER 3

Contemporary Perspectives on Bioethics

The Possibility of Designer Babies Raises Ethical Questions

Stephen L. Baird

Stephen L. Baird is a technology teacher at Bayside Middle School in Virginia Beach, Virginia, and an adjunct faculty member at Old Dominion University.

"Designer babies" is a popular term used to describe reproductive technologies that give parents the ability to make choices about the traits of their offspring. In the following viewpoint Baird explains that some of these technologies are relatively uncontroversial—for instance, in vitro fertilization. Other technologies include the manipulation of cell structure and the mapping of the human genome that will make it possible to screen embryos for certain diseases, select the sex of a baby, or to select certain desirable traits. Baird warns that these advances bring with them potential ethical issues that need to be carefully weighed by parents and physicians.

Almost three decades ago, on July 25, 1978, Louise Brown, the first "test-tube baby" was born. The world's first "test-tube" baby arrived amid a storm of protest and hand-wringing about science gone amok, human-animal hybrids, and the rebirth of eugenics. But the voices of those opposed to the procedure were silenced when Brown was born. She was a happy, healthy infant, and her parents were thrilled. The doctors who helped to create her, Patrick Steptoe and Robert Edwards, could not have been more pleased. She was the first person ever created outside a woman's body and was as natural

Stephen L. Baird, "Designer Babies: Eugenics Repackaged or Consumer Options?" *The Technology Teacher*, vol. 66, no. 7, April 2007, pp. 12–16. Copyright © 2007 International Technology Education Association. Reproduced by permission.

baby as had ever entered the world. Today in vitro fertilization (IVF) is often the unremarkable choice of tens of thousands of infertile couples whose only complaint is that the procedure is too difficult, uncertain, and expensive. What was once so deeply disturbing now seems to many people just another part of the modern world. Will the same be said one day of children with genetically enhanced intelligence, endurance, and other traits? Or will such attempts—if they occur at all—lead to extraordinary problems that are looked back upon as the ultimate in twenty-first century hubris?

Profound Consequences

Soon we may be altering the genes of our children to engineer key aspects of their character and physiology. The ethical and social consequences will be profound. We are standing at the threshold of an extraordinary, yet troubling, scientific dawn that has the potential to alter the very fabric of our lives, challenging what it means to be human, and perhaps redesigning our very selves. We are fast approaching the most consequential technological threshold in all of human history: the ability to alter the genes we pass to our children. Genetic engineering is already being carried out successfully on nonhuman animals. The gene that makes jellyfish fluorescent has been inserted into mice embryos, resulting in glow-in-the-dark rodents. Other mice have had their muscle mass increased, or have been made to be more faithful to their partners, through the insertion of a gene into their normal genetic make-up. But this method of genetic engineering is thus far inefficient. In order to produce one fluorescent mouse, several go wrong and are born deformed. If human babies are ever to be engineered, the process would have to become far more efficient, as no technique involving the birth of severely defective human beings to create a "genetically enhanced being" will hopefully ever be tolerated by our society. Once humans begin genetically engineering their children for desired traits, we will have crossed a threshold of no return. The communities of the world are just beginning to understand the full implications of the new human genetic technologies. There are few civil society institutions, and there are no social or political movements, critically addressing the immense social, cultural, and psychological challenges these technologies pose.

Until recently, the time scale for measuring change in the biological world has been tens of thousands, if not millions of years, but today it is hard to imagine what humans may be like in a few hundred years. The forces pushing humanity toward attempts at self-modification, through biological and technological advances, are powerful, seductive ones that we will be hard-pressed to resist. Some will curse these new technologies, sounding the death knell for humanity, envisioning the social, cultural, and moral collapse of our society and perhaps our civilization. Others see the same technologies as the ability to take charge of our own evolution, to transcend human limitations, and to improve ourselves as a species. As the human species moves out of its childhood, it is time to acknowledge our technological capabilities and to take responsibility for them. We have little choice, as the reweaving of the fabric of our genetic makeup has already begun. . . .

Several Levels of Screening

The practice of human genetic engineering is considered by some to have had its beginnings with in vitro fertilization in 1978. IVF paved the way for preimplantation genetic diagnosis (PGD), also referred to as preimplantation genetic selection (PGS). PGD is the process by which an embryo is microscopically examined for signs of genetic disorders. Several genetically based diseases can now be identified, such as Down Syndrome, Tay-Sachs Disease, Sickle Cell Anemia, Cystic Fibrosis, and Huntington's disease. There are many others that can be tested for, and both medical and scientific institutes are constantly searching for and developing new tests. For these tests, no real genetic engineering is taking place; rather, single cells are removed from embryos using the same process as used during in vitro fertilization. These cells are then examined to identify which are carrying the genetic disorder and which are not. The embryos that have the genetic disorder are discarded, those that are free of the disorder are implanted into the woman's uterus in the hope that a baby will be born without the genetic disorder. This procedure is fairly uncontroversial except with those critics who argue that human life starts at conception and therefore the embryo is sacrosanct and should not be tampered with. Another use for this technique is gender selection, which is where the issue becomes slightly more controversial. Some disorders or diseases are gender-specific, so instead of testing for the disease or disorder, the gender of the embryo is determined and whichever gender is "undesirable" is discarded. This brings up ethical issues of gender selection and the consequences for the gender balance of the human species.

A more recent development is the testing of the embryos for tissue matching. The embryos are tested for a tissue match with a sibling that has already developed, or is in danger of developing, a genetic disease or disorder. The purpose is to produce a baby who can be a tissue donor. This type of procedure was successfully used to cure a six-year-old-boy of a rare blood disorder after transplanting cells from his baby brother, who was created to save him. Doctors say the technique could be used to help many other children with blood and metabolic disorders, but critics say creating a baby in order to treat a sick sibling raises ethical questions.

The child, Charlie Whitaker, from Derbyshire, England, was born with Diamond Blackfan Anemia, a condition that prevented him from creating his own red blood cells. He needed transfusions every three weeks and drug infusions nearly every night. His condition was cured by a transplant of cells from the umbilical cord of his baby brother Jamie, who was genetically selected to be a donor after his parents' embryos were screened to find one with a perfect tissue match. Three months after his transplant, Charlie's doctors said that he was cured of Diamond Blackfan Anemia, and the prognosis is that Charlie can now look forward to a normal quality of life. Is this the beginning of a slippery slope toward "designer" or "spare parts" babies, or is the result that there are now two healthy, happy children instead of one very sick child a justification to pursue and continue procedures such as this one? Policymakers and ethicists are just beginning to pay serious attention. A recent working paper by the President's Council on Bioethics noted that "as genomic knowledge increases and more genes are identified that correlate with diseases, the applications for PGD will likely increase greatly," including diagnosing and treating medical conditions such as cancer, mental illness, or asthma, and nonmedical traits such as temperament or height. "While currently a small practice," the Council's working paper declares, "PGD is a momentous development. It represents the first fusion of genomics and assisted reproduction—effectively opening the door to the genetic shaping of offspring.

In one sense PGD poses no new eugenic dangers. Genetic screening using amniocentesis has allowed parents to test the fitness of potential offspring for years. But PGD is poised to increase this power significantly: It will allow parents to choose the child they want, not simply reject the ones they do not want. It will change the overriding purpose of IVF, from a treatment for fertility to being able to pick and choose embryos like consumer goods—producing many, discarding most, and desiring only the chosen few.

The next step in disease elimination is to attempt to refine a process known as "human germline engineering" or "human germline modification." Whereas preimplantation genetic diagnosis (PGD) affects only the immediate offspring, germline engineering seeks to affect the genes that are carried in the ova and sperm, thus eliminating the disease or disorder from all future generations, making it no longer inheritable. The possibilities for germline engineering go beyond the elimination of disease and open the door for modifications to human longevity, increased intelligence, increased muscle mass, and many other types of genetic enhancements. This application is by far the more consequential, because it opens the door to the alteration of the human species. The modified genes would appear not only in any children that resulted from such procedures, but in all succeeding generations. . . .

Proponents of germline manipulation assume that once a gene implicated in a particular condition is identified, it might be appropriate and relatively easy to replace, change, supplement, or otherwise modify that gene. However, biological characteristics or traits usually depend on interactions among many genes and, more importantly, the activity of genes is affected by various processes that occur both inside the organism and in its surroundings. This means that scientists cannot predict the full effect that any gene modification will have on the traits of people or other organisms.

There is no universally accepted ideal of biological perfection. To make intentional changes in the genes that people will pass on to their descendants would require that we, as a society, agree on how to classify "good" and "bad" genes. We do not have the necessary criteria, nor are there mechanisms for establishing such measures. Any formulation of such criteria would inevitably reflect particular current social biases. The definition of the standards and the technological means for implementing them would largely be determined by economically and socially privileged groups.

Designer Babies Are Possible

"Designer babies" is a term used by journalists and commentators—not by scientists—to describe several different reproductive technologies. These technologies have one thing in common: they give parents more control over what their offspring will be like. Designer babies are made possible by progress in three fields:

1. *Advanced Reproductive Technologies.* In the decades since the first "test tube baby" was born, reproductive medicine has helped countless women conceive and bear children. Today there are hundreds of thousands of humans who were conceived thanks to in vitro fertilization. Other advanced reproductive technologies include frozen embryos, egg and sperm donations, surrogate motherhood, pregnancies by older women, and the direct injection of a sperm cell into an egg.

2. *Cell and Chromosome Manipulation.* The past decade has seen astonishing breakthroughs in our knowledge of cell structure. Our ability to transfer chromosomes (the long threads of DNA in each cell) has led to major developments in cloning. Our knowledge of stem cells will make many new therapies possible. As we learn more about how reproduction works at the cellular level, we will gain more control over the earliest stages of a baby's development.

3. *Genetics and Genomics.* With the mapping of the human genome, our understanding of how DNA affects human development is only just beginning. Someday we might be able to switch bits of DNA on or off as we wish, or replace sections of DNA at will; research in that direction is already well underway.

Human reproduction is a complex process. There are many factors involved in the reproduction process: the genetic constitution of the parents, the condition of the parents' egg and sperm, and the health and behavior of the impregnated mother. When you consider the enormous complexity of the human genome, with its billions of DNA pairs, it becomes clear that reproduction will always have an element of unpredictability. To a certain extent we have always controlled our children's characteristics through the selection of mates. New technologies will give us more power to influence our children's "design"—but our control will be far from total.

Since the term "designer babies" is so imprecise, it is difficult to untangle its various meanings so as to make judgments about which techniques are acceptable. Several different techniques have been discussed, such as screening embryos for high-risk diseases, selecting the sex of a baby, picking an embryo for specific traits, genetic manipulation for therapeutic reasons, and genetic manipulation for cosmetic reasons. Although, to date, none of these techniques are feasible, recent scientific breakthroughs and continued work by the scientific community will eventually make each a possibility in the selection process for the best possible embryo for implantation.

Arguments for Designer Babies

1. Using whatever techniques are available to help prevent certain genetic diseases will protect children from suffering debilitating diseases and deformities and reduce the financial and emotional strain on the parents. If we want the best for our children, why shouldn't we use the technology?

2. The majority of techniques available today can only be used by parents who need the help of fertility clinics to have children; since they are investing so much time and money in their effort to have a baby, shouldn't they be entitled to a healthy one?

3. A great many naturally conceived embryos are rejected from the womb for defects; by screening embryos, we are doing what nature would normally do for us.

4. Imagine the reaction nowadays if organ transplantation were to be prohibited because it is "unnatural"—even though that is what some people called for when transplantation was a medical novelty. It is hard to see how the replacement of a defective gene is any less "natural" than the replacement of a defective organ. The major difference is the entirely beneficial one that medical intervention need occur only once around the time of conception, and the benefits would be inherited by the child and its descendants.

Arguments Against Designer Babies

1. We could get carried away "correcting" perfectly healthy babies. Once we start down the slippery slope of eliminating embryos because they are diseased, what is to stop us from picking babies for their physical or psychological traits?

2. There is always the looming shadow of eugenics. This was the motivation for some government policies in Europe and the United States in the first half of the twentieth century that included forced sterilizations, selective breeding, and "racial hygiene." Techniques that could be used for designing babies will give us dangerous new powers to express our genetic preferences.

3. There are major social concerns—such as: Will we breed a race of super humans who look down on those without genetic enhancements? Will these new technologies only be available to the wealthy—resulting in a lower class that will still suffer from inherited diseases and disabilities? Will discrimination against people already born with disabilities increase if they are perceived as genetically inferior?

4. Tampering with the human genetic structure might actually have unintended and unpredictable consequences that could damage the gene pool.

5. Many of the procedures related to designing babies involve terminating embryos; many disapprove of this on moral and religious grounds.

As our technical abilities progress, citizens will have to cope with the ethical implications of designer babies, and governments will have to define a regulatory course. We will have to answer some fundamental questions: How much power should parents and doctors have over the design of their children? How much power should governments have over parents and doctors? These decisions should be made based on facts and on our social beliefs.

Stem Cell Research Opens Up
New Opportunities

The Philadelphia Inquirer

Founded in 1829, The Philadelphia Inquirer *is a daily morning newspaper serving the Philadelphia, Pennsylvania, metropolitan area.*

This editorial from The Philadelphia Inquirer *asserts that by reversing former president George W. Bush's ban on the use of federal funds for human embryonic stem cell research, President Barack Obama is restoring science to its correct place in public policy. It cites advocates of stem cell research to say the lifting of this ban offers the promise of cures for diseases and conditions including Parkinson's disease, paralysis, and heart disease.*

Americans are understandably divided over President Obama's decision to lift restrictions on federal funding of human embryonic stem-cell research. But he took the course that promises the greater medical benefit.

In reversing a funding ban imposed by President Bush, Obama yesterday also took a welcome step toward restoring the rightful place of scientific research in guiding public policy.

Obama's presidential order is expected to boost research that advocates believe could develop cures for afflictions from Parkinson's disease to paralysis to heart disease. He acknowledged the difficult moral questions that are raised but added, "As a person of faith, I believe we are called to care for each other and work to ease human suffering."

Embryonic stem cells can morph into any cell of the body. In August 2001, Bush banned federal funding for research into stem lines created after that date. His order restricted taxpayer dollars to only the 21 stem-cell lines or "colonies" that had been produced up to that time.

Opponents of embryonic stem-cell research say it is immoral because the days-old embryos are destroyed to create the stem-cell lines. But as noted by University of Pennsylvania medical ethicist Arthur Caplan, nearly all of the approximately 600,000 human embryos now in storage in the United States would be destroyed eventually, regardless. Only 70 embryo adoptions took place nationally last year.

Although embryos are a very early form of human life, not all embryos develop to infancy. It would be a lost opportunity for the rest of humankind not to use embryos that would otherwise be destroyed to save lives.

Obama's order doesn't address a separate legislative ban, which doesn't allow federal money to be spent for the development of new stem-cell lines. But that order does permit taxpayer dollars to be spent for research on lines that were created without federal funding.

"It opens up the ability to work on a broader range of lines," said Martin Grumet, director of the Rutgers Stem Cell Research Center. "It opens up new opportunities."

In 2005, New Jersey became the first state to finance research using embryonic stem cells, including lines prohibited from use in research receiving federal funding. But the state eliminated nearly all funding for research this year to balance its budget. Grumet said his team is applying for grants from the economic-stimulus legislation.

New stem-cell lines created since the Bush ban are said by scientists to be healthier and to have a better potential for treating diseases.

Another objection to embryonic research is that progress has been made using adult stem cells, which do not require the destruction of embryos. While that field holds promise, many scientists agree that research should occur using both strategies. To close one avenue is to shut off a field of vast potential without knowing the possible results.

The previous administration misused science to serve political goals. Obama's directive helps to separate ideology from scientific inquiry.

Stem Cell Research Is Important but Needs Restrictions

Charles Krauthammer

Charles Krauthammer is a syndicated columnist based in Washington, D.C., and a former member of the President's Council on Bioethics.

In the following viewpoint Krauthammer explains why he refused the invitation of the Obama administration to attend the signing ceremony overturning President George W. Bush's ban on embryonic stem cell research. While Krauthammer supports stem cell research in certain cases, he is highly critical of the Obama executive order for its lack of specificity. Lines need to be drawn—human embryos should not be created solely for the purpose of research, Krauthammer claims. The Obama executive order abdicates moral responsibility to scientists.

Last week, the White House invited me to a signing ceremony overturning the Bush (43) executive order on stem cell research. I assume this was because I have long argued in these columns and during my five years on the President's Council on Bioethics that, contrary to the Bush policy, federal funding should be extended to research on embryonic stem cell lines derived from discarded embryos in fertility clinics.

I declined to attend. Once you show your face at these things you become a tacit endorser of whatever they spring. My caution was vindicated.

President Bush had restricted federal funding for embryonic stem cell research to cells derived from embryos that had already been destroyed (as of his speech of Aug. 9, 2001).

While I favor moving that moral line to additionally permit the use of spare fertility clinic embryos, President Obama replaced it with no line at all. He pointedly left open the creation of cloned—and noncloned sperm-and-egg-derived—human embryos solely for the purpose of dismemberment and use for parts.

I am not religious. I do not believe that personhood is conferred upon conception. But I also do not believe that a human embryo is the moral equivalent of a hangnail and deserves no more respect than an appendix. Moreover, given the protean power of embryonic manipulation, the temptation it presents to science and the well-recorded human propensity for evil even in the pursuit of good, lines must be drawn. I suggested the bright line prohibiting the deliberate creation of human embryos solely for the instrumental purpose of research—a clear violation of the categorical imperative not to make a human life (even if only a potential human life) a means rather than an end.

On this, Obama has nothing to say. He leaves it entirely to the scientists. This is more than moral abdication. It is acquiescence to the mystique of "science" and its inherent moral benevolence. How anyone as sophisticated as Obama can believe this within living memory of Mengele and Tuskegee and the fake (and coercive) South Korean stem cell research is hard to fathom.

That part of the ceremony, watched from the safe distance of my office, made me uneasy. The other part—the ostentatious issuance of a memorandum on "restoring scientific integrity to government decision-making"—would have made me walk out.

Restoring? The implication, of course, is that while Obama is guided solely by science, Bush was driven by dogma, ideology and politics.

What an outrage. Bush's nationally televised stem cell speech was the most morally serious address on medical eth-

Jessica Dias removes a new batch of embryonic stem cells to be worked on at the Wisconsin National Primate Research Center at the University Wisconsin-Madison. On March 9, 2009, President Barack Obama signed an order reversing the Bush administration's limits on human embryonic stem cell research, an order that could facilitate the development of human cloning projects. Darren Hauck/Getty Images.

ics ever given by an American president. It was so scrupulous in presenting the best case for both his view *and the contrary view* that until the last few minutes, the listener had no idea where Bush would come out.

Obama's address was morally unserious in the extreme. It was populated, as his didactic discourses always are, with a forest of straw men. Such as his admonition that we must resist the "false choice between sound science and moral values." Yet, exactly 2 minutes and 12 seconds later he went on to declare that he would never open the door to the "use of cloning for human reproduction."

Does he not think that a cloned human would be of extraordinary scientific interest? And yet he banned it.

Is he so obtuse as not to see that he had just made a choice of ethics over science? Yet, unlike Bush, who painstakingly explained the balance of ethical and scientific goods he was trying to achieve, Obama did not even pretend to make the case why some practices are morally permissible and others not.

This is not just intellectual laziness. It is the moral arrogance of a man who continuously dismisses his critics as ideological while he is guided exclusively by pragmatism (in economics, social policy, foreign policy) and science in medical ethics.

Science has everything to say about what is possible. Science has nothing to say about what is permissible. Obama's pretense that he will "restore science to its rightful place" and make science, not ideology, dispositive in moral debates is yet more rhetorical sleight of hand—this time to abdicate decision-making and color his own ideological preferences as authentically "scientific."

Dr. James Thomson, the pioneer of embryonic stem cells, said "if human embryonic stem cell research does not make you at least a little bit uncomfortable, you have not thought about it enough." Obama clearly has not.

Genetic Research Poses a
Threat to Civil Liberties

Philip L. Bereano

Philip L. Bereano is a professor in the Department of Human Centered Design and Engineering at the University of Washington. He serves on the national board of directors of the American Civil Liberties Union and is a founder of the Council for Responsible Genetics.

While advances in genetic research offer the potential to eliminate or mitigate certain diseases or conditions and thus improve the overall quality of life, Bereano submits in the following selection that these advances also bring with them some significant threats to our civil liberties. For example, genetic screening can be used by individuals to make decisions about their own health; however, it can also be used by insurance companies to deny coverage to people with certain conditions.

The Human Gene Project at the National Institutes of Health, also being supported in universities all across America, will one day in the not-too-distant future enable every set of parents that has a little baby to get a map of the genetic structure of their child. So if their child has a predisposition to a certain kind of illness or a certain kind of problem, or even to heart disease or stroke in the early 40's, they will be able to plan that child's life, that child's upbringing, to minimize the possibility of the child developing that illness or that predisposition, to organize the diet plan, the exercise plan, the medical treatment that would enable untold numbers of people to have far more full lives than would have been the case before...

[Former President Bill Clinton]

Philip L. Bereano, "Does Genetic Research Threaten Our Civil Liberties?" *Action bioscience.org*, August 2000. Copyright © 2000, American Institute of Biological Sciences. Reproduced by permission.

However, the confluence of a number of technical and social trends has greatly enhanced the capacity for using genetic techniques for surveillance and tracking:

• The science of genetics is a flourishing new industry, nourished in large part by the federally funded Human Genome Project. The goal of this ambitious research endeavor is to identify every gene found in the human body, perhaps 100,000 in all. Several months ago [in early 2000], the U.S. government and a private corporation announced that they had "completed" the "map" of the genome, although actually there are still many gaps. Much related research focuses on genetic diagnostics—tests designed to identify genes thought to be associated with various medical conditions. More than 50 new genetic tests have been identified in the past five years alone.

• The increasing speed, sophistication, affordability, and interconnectivity of computer systems allows the rapid monitoring and matching of many millions of records. A 1994 benchmark study by the ACLU [American Civil Liberties Union] found that "concerns about personal privacy run deep among the American people."

• The promotion of an ideology of geneticization fosters the belief that genes are determinative of an individual's behavior, character, and future.

• Capitalist economic relations have created a scramble for venture capital, the altering of patent laws, and calls for mass genetic testing by researchers who trade on the old image of the altruistic scientist to mask their conflicts of interest in testing labs, patents, consulting contracts, etc.

Technologies Not Value-Neutral

Technologies are not value-neutral; they usually embody the perspectives, purposes, and political objectives of powerful social groups. The dominant ideology in Western society proclaims that science and technology are value-neutral, and the only problems caused by technologies are either "externalities" (unintended side effects) or abuses. However, because technologies are the result of human interventions into the otherwise natural progression of activities (and not acts of God or of nature), they are themselves actually imbued with human intentions and purposes. Current technologies do not equally benefit all segments of society (and indeed are not intended to do so), although to maximize public support for these developments and to minimize potential opposition, their proponents rarely acknowledge these distributional ramifications.

The United States is a society in which the differential access to wealth and power has been exacerbated during recent years. Thus, those people with more power can determine the kinds of technological developments that are researched and implemented. Because of their size, scale, and requirements for capital investments and for knowledge, modern technologies are powerful interventions into the natural order. They tend to be the mechanisms by which already powerful groups extend, manifest, and further consolidate their powers. Thus, technologies themselves are not neutral; they are social and political phenomena. Genetic technologies and computerization exhibit these characteristics, and reflect power differentials in our society.

The resulting milieu of technological triumphalism appears to offer omniscience—capabilities of enhanced surveillance and control over people and events, as well as promises of perfectionism (thus leading to both a loss of privacy and increased opportunities for discrimination by powerful entities). Predictability will replace a tolerance for natural variation and diversity. Powerful scientists have already called for programs of eugenics, labeled as "genetic enhancement" to create a less distasteful package.

Loss of Privacy a Real Concern

Genetic privacy, like medical privacy in general, involves notions of the dignity and integrity of the individual. Is data accurate; can individuals access their own files; can the donor correct inaccurate data; are the custodians faithful and are technical security systems protecting the data where possible; does the individual have control over which third parties are allowed access, and under what conditions?

• The US Department of Defense insists on taking DNA samples from all its personnel, ostensibly for identification of those killed in action and body parts from military accidents—despite the fact that the samples are to be kept for 50 years (long after people have left active duty), the program includes civilian employees, the agency refuses to issue regulations barring all third party use, and the Department will not accept waivers from the next of kin of subjects not wanting to donate tissues.

• The FBI has been promoting the genetic screening of criminals to establish state DNA identification data banks to be used in criminal investigations; indeed, Federal legislation penalizes states fiscally if they don't participate, and now all do. Yet the data includes samples from those whose crimes have low recidivism rates or don't leave tissue samples; in some states people merely accused are forced into the program, and in others there are politicians calling for an expansion along these lines, despite the Constitutional presumption of innocence.

• Infant blood samples, from the heel-sticks used to determine blood type and test for PKU [phenylketonuria] are stored as "Guthrie blots." California alone has more than seven million in its repository.

The American Civil Liberties Union advocates that "the decision to undergo genetic screening is purely personal" and it should not be "subject to control or compulsion by third parties" or the government. And "where a person has intentionally undergone genetic screening procedures there must be no disclosure of findings to third parties without the express and informed consent of the subject given after the results of the screening are made known to the subject and upon such times and conditions as the subject may require . . ."

Yet patients' records "are commodities for sale," in the words of the *New York Times* a few years ago, and a panel of the US National Research Council has warned that the computerized medical records of millions of citizens are open to misuse and abuse.

Genetic Discrimination

Genetic discrimination is the other major civil liberty threatened by genetics research. Scientists working with the Council for Responsible Genetics [CRG] have documented hundreds of cases where healthy people have been denied insurance or employment based on genetic "predictions." Of course, relatively few genetic diseases are deterministic; most tests (which have inherent limits themselves) cannot tell us if a genetic mutation will become manifest; if it does do so, it cannot tell us when in life this will occur; and if it happens, how severe the condition will be. In addition, many genetic conditions can be controlled or treated by interventions and environmental changes; that is why governments mandate testing newborns for PKU.

The growth of the mania for testing in the US is a manifestation of class relationships, through new technological possibilities: employers test employees, insurance companies and health organizations test patients, college officials test students, legislators pass bills to test a variety of disempowered groups (welfare recipients, prisoners, immigrants and the like). Such indignities are never foisted upon the ruling class by the masses.

Examples of such discrimination include:

• A pregnant woman, whose fetus tested positive for cystic fibrosis, was told by her health maintenance organization (HMO) that it would be willing to cover the cost of an abortion but would not cover the infant under the family's medical policy if she elected to carry the pregnancy to term.

• A healthy woman, who casually mentioned to her family doctor that her father had been diagnosed with Huntington's disease, and that she herself was at risk for inheriting this genetic disorder, was later denied disability insurance. The insurance company rejected her because they found a note about her father's diagnosis written in the margin of her medical records.

• A healthy boy, who carried a gene predisposing him to a heart disorder, was denied health coverage by his parents' insurance company, even though the boy took medication that eliminated his risk of heart disease.

• One healthy man in his 20s with a gene for the degenerative brain condition Huntington's disease was refused life insurance. His older brother, on the other hand, tested negative and was able to reduce his premium which had been previously set on a family history of the disease.

• Another case involved a well woman in her 30s whose genetic test indicated a 70 to 90 per cent risk of developing cancer. Despite having regular screening for cancer, her superannuation was reduced and the life component refused.

Higher Premiums

Federal legislation, the Health Insurance Portability and Accountability Act (HIPAA, 1996), limits genetic discrimination as a basis for denying certain medical insurance policies, but it does not prohibit charging higher premiums, nor does it cover life, disability, or automobile insurance or employment—all areas of documented discrimination. Slowly, state by state, the CRG, ACLU, and patients' rights groups are trying to get legislation passed to reduce or eliminate genetic discrimination; about 40 states have enacted some type of protections, but many are very weak and/or partial.

Federal rules for medical privacy (including genetic information) under HIPAA were announced in August 2000, after weaker proposals by the Clinton Administration received a great deal of criticism. While providing standards for the disclosure of bio-information, the rules require that the patient only receive notice, not give consent; thus, there still would not be full patient control over sensitive information.

The President [Clinton] has also announced his support of a Federal bill which would prohibit health insurance providers from using any type of genetic information for making decisions about whether to cover a person or what premium to charge. This legislation would address some of the discrimination problems which have been occurring. And he has issued an Executive Order barring genetic discrimination in Federal employment.

Social and Environmental Factors

Beyond the risks of discrimination and loss of privacy, however, society's fascination with genetic determinism has other social and political consequences. An overemphasis on the role of genes in human health neglects environmental and social factors, thus contributing to the image of people with "defective" genes as "damaged goods." This, in effect, encourages a "blame the victim" mindset, directly contrary to the public policy embodied in the Americans with Disabilities Act [passed in 1990]. Economic and social resources end up being diverted into finding biomedical "solutions" while societal measures get short-changed.

Although new technologies claim to offer us more "freedom," they really can threaten our civic values. This is certainly true of the new biology. As [Thomas] Jefferson warned, "the price of liberty is eternal vigilance"—it isn't genetically hard-wired to happen automatically.

For Further Discussion

1. In Chapter 1 Johan Heje writes that Aldous Huxley is a novelist of ideas and that his novels are fictionalized versions of the essays that he wrote throughout his life, expounding on the social and political themes that were important to him. What are some of the themes Huxley is conveying in *Brave New World*?

2. In Chapter 2 John Derbyshire argues that *Brave New World* is no longer relevant, calling it a "period piece." Do you think *Brave New World* is still relevant today? Why or why not?

3. In Chapter 2 Leon R. Kass contends that Huxley accurately predicted many of the biotechnological advances that are a reality today, such as cloning, genetic screening, and in vitro fertilization. Kass also writes that Huxley was on the mark in foretelling that these technological advances would bring with them cultural changes. Do you agree with Kass's position, especially that these advances are coming at the price of a lack of freedom? Give specifics to support your position.

4. In Chapter 3 the editors of *The Philadelphia Inquirer* and Charles Krauthammer disagree about stem cell research. The *Philadelphia Inquirer* editorial supports President Barack Obama's reversal of the ban on the use of federal funds for stem cell research, while Krauthhammer argues that there must be additional guidelines. Knowing what you know of Huxley, which position do you think he would support? Give reasons.

5. In Chapter 3 Stephen L. Baird suggests that the ability to make choices about the traits of offspring poses ethical issues that need to be addressed by parents and the medical profession. What are some of these issues?

For Further Reading

M.T. Anderson, *Feed*. Cambridge, MA: Candlewick Press, 2002.

Margaret Atwood, *The Handmaid's Tale*. Toronto: McClelland and Stewart, 1985.

———, *Oryx and Crake*. New York: Nan A. Talese, 2003.

Ray Bradbury, *Fahrenheit 451*. New York: Ballantine, 1953.

Anthony Burgess, *A Clockwork Orange*. London: Heinemann, 1962.

William Golding, *Lord of the Flies*. London: Faber, 1954.

Robert A. Heinlein, *Stranger in a Strange Land*. New York: Putnam, 1961.

Aldous Huxley, *Brave New World Revisited*. New York: Harper, 1958.

———, *Island*. New York: Harper, 1962.

Kazuo Ishiguro, *Never Let Me Go*. New York: Knopf, 2005.

Ken Kesey, *One Flew over the Cuckoo's Nest*. New York: Viking, 1962.

Lois Lowry, *The Giver*. Boston: Houghton Mifflin, 1993.

George Orwell, *Animal Farm*. New York: Harcourt, Brace, 1946.

———, *Nineteen Eighty-Four*. New York: Harcourt, Brace, 1949.

Kurt Vonnegut, Jr., *Slaughterhouse-Five; or, The Children's Crusade: A Duty-Dance with Death*. New York: Dell, 1969.

Evelyn Waugh, *Love Among the Ruins: A Romance of the Near Future*. London: Chapman & Hall, 1953.

Scott Westerfeld, *Uglies*. New York: Simon Pulse, 2005.

Yevgeny Zamyatin, *We*. New York: Dutton, 1924.

Bibliography

Books

David Bradshaw   *The Hidden Huxley*. Boston: Faber & Faber, 1994.

E.J. Brown   *"Brave New World," "1984," and "We": An Essay on Anti-Utopia*. Ann Arbor, MI: Ardis, 1976.

Francis Fukuyama   *Our Posthuman Future: Consequences of the Biotechnology Revolution*. New York: Farrar, Straus & Giroux, 2002.

Jonathan Glover   *Choosing Children: Genes, Disability, and Design*. New York: Oxford University Press, 2006.

Alexander Henderson   *Aldous Huxley*. New York: Russell & Russell, 1964.

Eve Herold   *Stem Cell Wars: Inside Stories from the Frontlines*. New York: Palgrave Macmillan, 2006.

Julian Huxley, ed.   *Aldous Huxley, 1894–1963: A Memorial Volume*. New York: Harper & Row, 1965.

Laura Archera Huxley   *This Timeless Moment: A Personal View of Aldous Huxley*. New York: Farrar, Straus & Giroux, 1968.

David Garrett Izzo and Kim Kirkpatrick, eds.   *Huxley's "Brave New World": Essays*. Jefferson, NC: McFarland, 2008.

Robert E. Kuehn, ed.	*Aldous Huxley: A Collection of Critical Essays.* Englewood Cliffs, NJ: Prentice-Hall, 1974.
Keith May	*Aldous Huxley.* New York: Barnes & Noble, 1972.
Nicholas Murray	*Aldous Huxley: A Biography.* New York: Thomas Dunne Books/St. Martin's Press, 2002.
Gregory Stock	*Redesigning Humans: Choosing Our Genes, Changing Our Future.* Boston: Houghton Mifflin, 2003.
Philip Thody	*Aldous Huxley: A Biographical Introduction.* New York: Scribner's, 1973.
Ian Wilmut and Roger Highfield	*After Dolly: The Uses and Misuses of Human Cloning.* New York: Norton, 2006.

Periodicals

Bernard Bergonzi	"Life's Divisions: The Continuing Debate on Aldous Huxley," *Encounter,* July 1973.
Jane Bosveld	"Evolution by Design," *Discover,* March 2009.
Christian Century	"Stem Cell Advance May Not End Debate," December 25, 2007.
Margaret Cheney Dawson	"Huxley Turns Propagandist," *New York Herald Tribune Book Review,* February 7, 1932.

David King
Dunaway

"Huxley and Human Cloning: *Brave New World* in the Twenty-first Century," *Aldous Huxley Annual: A Journal of Twentieth-Century Thought and Beyond*, vol. 2, 2002.

Michael Fumento

"No, the Stem Cell Debate Is Not Over," *American Spectator*, April 2008.

William Harless

"Who's Afraid of a Brave New World?" *Boulevard*, Fall 2004.

Henry Hazlitt

"What's Wrong with Utopia?" *Nation*, February 17, 1932.

Granville Hicks

"Three Books by Aldous Huxley," *New Republic*, February 10, 1932.

Martin Kessler

"Power and the Perfect State: A Study in Disillusionment as Reflected in Orwell's *Nineteen Eighty-Four* and Huxley's *Brave New World*," *Political Science Quarterly*, December 1957.

Matthew Killeya

"Insider: Biotechnology Under the Spotlight," *New Scientist*, May 3, 2008.

Jeffrey J. Kripal

"Brave New Worldview," *Chronicle of Higher Education*, December 12, 2008.

Edward Lobb

"The Subversion of Drama in Huxley's *Brave New World*," *International Fiction Review*, Summer 1984.

Gene McQuillan   "The Politics of Allusion: *Brave New World* and the Debates About Biotechnologies," *Studies in the Humanities*, June 2006.

Firuza R. Parikh   "Q: Will We Have Designer Babies in the Future? A: Yes, but Technology Should Be Used Responsibly," *India Today*, December 18, 2006.

Nicholas von Hoffman   "Huxley Vindicated," *Spectator*, July 17, 1982.

Index

W

Ward, Mrs. Humphrey, 24, 46
Watson, John B., 111–112
Watts, Harold H., 45–57
Wells, H.G., 23, 25–26, 63, 84,
  122–123, 126
West, Rebecca, 109–115

Whitaker, Charlie, 131–132
Wittgenstein, Ludwig, 68–69
Women, 86–94
Woodcock, George, 95–103

Z

Zavos, Panayiotis M., *81*